How to Fake Your Way through a

Wine List

**Tips and Tricks
to Sound Like
an Expert**

Katherine Cole

STERLING EPICURE
New York

STERLING EPICURE
New York

An Imprint of Sterling Publishing
1166 Avenue of the Americas
New York, NY 10036

ISBN 978-1-4549-1603-1

Distributed in Canada by Sterling Publishing
c/o Canadian Manda Group, 664 Annette Street
Toronto, Ontario, Canada M6S 2C8

For information about custom editions, special sales,
and premium and corporate purchases, please contact
Sterling Special Sales at 800-805-5489 or
specialsales@sterlingpublishing.com.

This book was designed and produced by
Fine Wine Editions Ltd.
6 Blundell Street
London N7 9BH

Project Editor: Hilary Lumsden
Editorial Assistant: Juliet Lough
Designer: John Round
Illustrator: Alice Potter
Production Manager: Nikki Ingram

Editorial Director: Ruth Patrick
Publisher: Mark Fletcher

Manufactured in China

2 4 6 8 10 9 7 5 3 1

www.sterlingpublishing.com

"With all these books, as with any on the subject, do not expect to turn yourself into an expert via the printed word alone ... Reading must be combined with as much drinking experience as pocket and liver will allow."

Kingsley Amis, *On Drink*

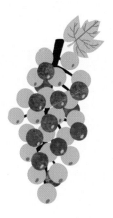

CONTENTS

INTRODUCTION

Pity the doctor at the cocktail party. When people hear what she does for a living, they start telling the poor physician about their irritable bowels and arthritis pains. This is not what a person wants to hear about after work on a Friday night. I, too, am guilty of cornering medical professionals in social situations to talk about my food allergies and my kids' adenoids and ear infections. I'm not proud of it. And I should know better.

Because the same thing has happened to me over my many years of working as a wine writer. Just to be clear, I didn't go to medical school. I didn't swear to the Hippocratic Oath. I don't save peoples' lives. I just write irrelevant stories about a tasty alcoholic beverage. And then complain about parties. I know: First World problems.

But, getting back to it. In social situations, when people hear what I do, their eyes grow wide. And then the standard script rolls:

"Oh, wow. I don't know much about wine. I'd be so embarrassed to order wine with you."
RESPONSE *"On behalf of my profession, I apologize. Wine is supposed to be relaxing and pleasurable. If it's a source of embarrassment for you, the entire purpose of wine has been defeated. Please, just have fun with it."*

"What's your favorite wine?"
RESPONSE *"I don't have one favorite wine. I crave a different wine for every occasion and mood. How long have you got?"*

"To be honest, I've got a couple of wine books and I even subscribed to a wine magazine for a while, but it's all just so overwhelming. I'm trying to learn more about the wines I know

I like, but there's just so much information—grapes, regions, villages ...."

RESPONSE *"I feel your pain. I'm working on a book for you. It's all about how to fake your way through a wine list."*

As I write this, I am vexed with my profession. Why do we describe wines as "angular due to the lack of ML?" Who in their right mind writes tasting notes that suggest a food match of foie gras? Why do our descriptions of Barbaresco fail to mention that Barbaresco is a place and the name of the grape is actually Nebbiolo?

Why do wine writers act like we're all from the planet Krikkit, completely out of touch with the rest of the universe? Don't we know that people are busy and mostly subscribe to wine publications because they look good on their coffee tables? Are we on a mission to turn fully functioning, successful adults into neurotics with inferiority complexes?

Time to offer some answers. I wish I could boil the whole wine world down into a concise and simple statement that you could fit into a text message. But that's like saying that the answer to the ultimate question of life, the universe, and everything is forty-two. It doesn't do the universe justice.

This book is all I can offer for now. It's for those of you who want to dig a little deeper into the world of wine. It's not exhaustive, but it's fairly detailed. You can take as much or as little from it as you'd like. If you can find just two or three wine styles that suit you and commit a few salient facts about them to memory, you'll find that dinners out and visits to wine shops get a lot easier. Cocktail parties, too.

And at that next cocktail party, thank that doctor for all she does, then get her a glass of wine.

Chapter One

TAKE THE
FIRST STEPS

You've finally done it: You've admitted you are not an expert on wine. In fact, you don't know much about it at all. Everyone else seems to know their Shiraz from their Syrah and their Grigio from their Gris. But you needn't feel perplexed. Because you are not alone. And you're in a safe place. So let's start this journey of empowerment together.

GET INTO THE MINDSET

Oh, no. Here he comes. It's the sommelier. And he's carrying what looks like the Gutenberg Bible. It's big, heavy, and leather-bound, anyway. He stops at your table and hands the monstrous thing to you. Your thirsty dining companions—visiting family or important clients— all stare at you expectantly. You begin to leaf through the oversized pages in an increasingly agitated state of panic.

Wine is supposed to be relaxing and enjoyable. So why do we feel like we're nervous college students, preparing for a final exam, every time we're faced with a restaurant wine list? Who are those smug connoisseurs who waltz into a wine shop and begin bantering with the owner in a foreign-sounding language? What do they know and how do they know it?

Most of us believe that wine is an exclusive club that we haven't been invited to join. We're under the impression we can't possibly choose a wine until we've memorized the name of every village in Burgundy. Why? Because wine books tend to be thick compendiums of maps, vintages, symbols, and fine print, and many wine aficionados speak in an inscrutable code, as though they are part of some secret society.

> Most of us believe that wine is an exclusive club that we haven't been invited to join.

EVERYONE STARTS OUT A BEGINNER

But consider this: The world's most admired wine experts were once just like you. Sara Schneider, the wine editor of *Sunset* magazine, works a short drive from California's world-renowned Napa Valley and Sonoma County. But—under duress—she admits that she spent her early twenties drinking sweet, pink wine. "I thought a friend was just wrong when he served me a red wine and

DESSERT (BRAC...
...VIRA-BIRBET (BRAC...
...NGAROTTI VINO SANTO
...ETTA MOSCATO PASSITO   6.50
...T HAZELNUT SHERRY   6.00
...O CHOCOLATE PORT   6.00
...E CHIARLO_BAROLO CHINATO
(Piedmontese elixir) 10.00

RAMO...
GRAHAM'S ...
FONSECA 20 YE...
DOW'S   VINTA...
GRAHAM'S V...
WARRE'S   VIN...
TAYLOR FLAI...

called it 'Zinfandel,'" she recalls. She remembers retorting contentiously that, "Zinfandel is pink."

"It wasn't until I took introductory wine classes much later in culinary school that the full extent of my ignorance dawned on me," Schneider says. "The deeper into wine I dive, even now, the more I know that I don't know."

Likewise, "I used to shudder when I was asked if I wanted 'Burgundy.'" recalls Leslie Sbrocco, wine author, television host, and resident wine expert for NBC's *Today* show. "I would roll my eyes thinking it was just a cheap, supermarket wine. What I later realized was true French Burgundy is one of the wine world's iconic regions and is home to the noble grapes Pinot Noir and Chardonnay. After nearly twenty years as a wine professional, I'm constantly building my wall of wine knowledge with every sip I take."

As an amateur wine enthusiast, Sbrocco realized that European wines are typically named for their regions, not

That chalkboard isn't an exam for which you haven't studied

the grape they're made from. So she came up with a concept she called "The Name Game," which matched grape variety names to the titles of their growing regions. By playing this game in her mind, she got herself up to speed.

Sbrocco tapped into a painless way of acquiring knowledge: If it feels like play rather than work, it sticks. Think about children who are good spellers. They don't try to memorize the dictionary. For the most part, they simply love to read. While they're flying on a broomstick with Harry Potter, those bookish youngsters are picking up vocabulary words without any awareness at all that they're learning.

SOME TRICKS FROM THE KIDS

Likewise, we've all heard about those kids who played pickup games of soccer in the street and then grew up to be great athletes. For these highly skilled technicians, exercise started out as recreation, not a chore. And what about those older students who score outstandingly on standardized tests? Sure, they study. But they also know how to "game" the system.

Like a spelling-bee winner, the budding wine aficionado can learn without trying to. And like the student who aces all the exams and scores big on the field, the successful junior wine enthusiast knows how to study smart—and have fun with it—rather than studying hard.

The best poker players know how to read facial expressions and calculate simple odds. Like a card shark, the wine amateur can trump the wine-selection game by employing the perfect combination of bluster, charm, and humility.

So let's make like spelling-bee champs and turn leisure activities into learning opportunities. And let's tap in to our inner grifters and pass ourselves off as suave connoisseurs. (Minus the life of crime, of course.)

The successful junior wine enthusiast knows how to study smart—and have fun with it—rather than studying hard.

DRINK WINE WHILE
READING THIS BOOK

Your first assignment: Pour yourself a glass of wine and get sipping. Wine makes everything—including reading about wine—more fun. But that's not only why I'm recommending that you break into a bottle. Rather, by making a subliminal connection to the material, you'll be employing a technique proven to make memories stick. Just be sure to sip slowly enough that your brain doesn't fog over.

There are other ways you can pump up your productivity by playing with your atmosphere. Have you ever noticed that, if you take your laptop to a café, you get a lot of work done, but when you're alone in your quiet office, you are the master of procrastination? It turns out that a bit of external stimulus—a cup of coffee, the buzz of conversation, the sight of people strolling by outside the window—helps your brain to focus. So in addition to pouring that glass of wine, turn on the stereo. And move around. Read this book on your sofa, in bed, in the bath, at a wine bar, even at the gym (without the glass of wine, unless your gym is more fun than mine.) Research has proven that the more we move around while studying, the more likely we are to retain information.

Finally, make your learning experience a social one. Create a winetasting group with friends in which you sample a different type of wine every month, like a book club. Or, simply open a bottle and talk about it with a buddy. You don't need to throw out snooty-sounding descriptors. Just vocalize whether you're enjoying the wine or not. By forming opinions and voicing them aloud, you'll be further embedding the wine in your personal file folder of knowledge.

Create a winetasting group with friends in which you sample a different type of wine every month, like a book club.

MAKE CONNECTIONS

How do avid sports fans remember every key play of a championship game? Why are film fanatics able to recall every line of a favorite movie? They have an inherent passion for the material. So connect your own passion with what you're learning about wine.

I nstead of trying to memorize a map of the wine regions of Chile and Argentina, for example, think of something that interests you and latch onto that instead. Say you're an avid skier or climber. You might enjoy figuring out which wine-producing regions are closest to the highest mountain peaks and best ski resorts in the Andes. Imagine treating yourself to a nice glass of wine from that region after a day spent on the slopes.

Too often, we try to remember the details about a wine without having a clear sense of where it came from. Just where is the Veneto, anyway? Can you picture it? If not, you probably won't remember which wines are made there. It's key to connect emotionally with the places our favorite wines come from. Just as the sound of an Edith Piaf song and the smell of a *croque monsieur* might remind you of that last trip to Paris, it helps to create a richly textured memory of sipping a Bellini on a Venetian piazza, with pigeons flapping about and a street musician playing a violin. Now you've got it … the Veneto is the region around the city of Venice and also the home of Prosecco, the sparkling wine in a Bellini cocktail.

To that end, chapter three will introduce an array of wine styles from seventy-five geographic locations all around the world. We'll delve into landmarks, customs, cuisines, and cultures to give you a sense of place and help you to visualize yourself in that setting. If you feel like you've been there, you're more likely to connect with the information. Of course, if you *have* been there, even better.

It's key to connect emotionally with the places our favorite wines come from.

Opposite: Wine's connection to place isn't merely one of climate and geography; culture and cuisine matter as well

BUILD A MEMORY PALACE

So we've learned how the spelling-bee champ and the childhood sports phenom might approach wine education. How about the straight-up, straight-A student? What do ace test-takers do that might help us with acquiring wine knowledge?

Here's where—yes—we do delve into some memorization. But it's *fun* memorization, I promise.

The Ancient Greek poet Simonides of Ceos receives credit for devising a memorization technique called the "memory palace." The premise is this: If you're trying to remember a list of words, start by visualizing a familiar place. Maybe it's your office building. Now, put one of those terms at each important signpost in that place. Place a memory at the bus stop outside, and another just inside the sliding doors. And another at the security guard's desk, and another in the elevator.

> You're tapping into the same technique we use for recalling driving or walking directions.

You're tapping into the same technique we use for recalling driving or walking directions: Take a right at the gas station, a left at the church, and so on. Except you're using your imagination to create directions to a memory.

But wait —there's more. If you've ever dabbled with a language-learning program or app, you might have noticed that associating an unfamiliar word with a familiar picture helps the term to stick in your mind. When we hear "*zapatos*" while viewing a picture of a pair of shoes, we'll remember those shoes the next time we hear that word.

So assign an image to each term you're trying to remember. Since many of the wine terms we'll be learning in this book are in foreign and unfamiliar languages, it's best to choose images that, if described, would rhyme or sound similar. Also, the more ridiculous and active the image, the stickier it will be in your mind. The cross-dressing cabal of General Franco, driving a Volkswagen Touareg to a dance club, makes Loire Valley red wine a lot more fun.

Simonides of Ceos, the father of mnemonics

Chapter three relies on mnemonics—like the "**cabal of General Franco**" for Cabernet Franc—to describe each new vocabulary word. It's up to you to link the salient terms together in a memory palace full of kooky images.

If you're a cat-lover, you may enjoy the following example, which plunges into the very depths of wine-memorization hell: The German classification system for indicating the relative richness of Riesling, called the "Prädikat." The ripeness levels range from Kabinett, the lightest, least-ripe style, to Spätlese, Auslese, Beerenauslese and finally Trockenbeerenauslese, the very sweetest, ripest, and richest style.

Non-German-speaking students might take one look at the previous paragraph and begin quietly weeping. But you won't, because you have this book to help you. So we're not going to worry about Prädikats. Instead, we're going to visualize a ***parade of cats***. (You can thank my mother, an avid crossword puzzler and word freak, for suggesting that image.)

The first cat, just inside your office building's doors, is crammed inside a narrow **cabinet** (Kabinett), just wide enough to store a coat and umbrella. The second is in the lobby, trying to squeeze into a slightly wider **space station** (Spätlese)—maybe it's just a space capsule—with **Reese Witherspoon** (she's blonde, brainy Riesling).

The third cat is in front of the elevators, curled up with Reese in a more tricked-out and spacious **outer** (Auslese) space station. The fourth is riding the elevator, along with a **bear** that's snacking on **berries**, also heading for **outer space** (Beerenauslese). The fifth cat can be found in the rooftop parking lot, piled in with a **truckload of bears**, again headed for **outer space** (Trockenbeerenauslese).

If you can remember that progression as a silly story, it will stick in your mind. The associative images and words I've chosen sound very much like the German pronunciations of the terms, so you don't have to stumble over how to say them. In fact, if you were to ask a sommelier to bring you the sort of German Riesling that sounds something like "outer space," they would know exactly what you were talking about.

You probably won't want to try to place any more images than that in a single memory palace at first. That's because it's easiest for us to remember things in small groups. Phone numbers, social security numbers, and credit card numbers are divided into chunks for just this reason.

Even if you're not setting out on a mission to stone-cold memorize, the mnemonic approach should make unfamiliar terms stick. And, if my suggestions aren't working for you, please feel free to substitute images that do resonate.

If you're interested in learning more about memorization strategies, I highly recommend you take a look at *Moonwalking with Einstein: The Art and Science of Remembering Everything* by Joshua Foer. The previous few paragraphs owe a deep debt to Foer's comprehensive and clear descriptions of the techniques used by world memory champions.

Speaking of enjoyment, that's enough blather from me. Now it's time for chapter two, in which we play a game.

Assign an image—the more outlandish the better—to each term you're trying to remember. It's best to choose one that rhymes or sounds similar.

Opposite: Use your creativity to remember complicated terms and concepts

Chapter Two

CHOOSE YOUR OWN WINE ADVENTURE

What's the most important question in wine? "Which one?" No! Try "When?" "With whom?" "What season? "What occasion?" "What are we eating?" Cross-reference your answers to these questions by consulting the following charts. By the end of your adventure, you should have found your wine, but your wine merchant can still help you fine-tune. Are you ready? Let's do this.

WHAT'S THE OCCASION?

WINES		SMALL DINNER PARTY	BIG CASUAL GROUP	ELEGANT COCKTAIL PARTY
DELICATE WHITE				
Washington Riesling	p.36		●	
New York Riesling	p.38	●		
Loire Chenin & Sauvignon Blanc	p.40			●
Gascony White Blend	p.42		●	
Mosel Riesling	p.44			●
Vaud & Valais Chasselas	p.46	●		
Friuli Pinot Grigio	p.48		●	
Marches Verdicchio	p.50	●		
Orvieto Trebbiano	p.52		●	
Galicia Albariño	p.54		●	
FULL-BODIED WHITE				
California Chardonnay	p.56			●
Casablanca Sauvignon Blanc	p.58		●	
Alsace Riesling	p.60			●
Burgundy Chardonnay	p.62	●		
Rhône White Blend	p.64			●
Wachau Grüner Veltliner	p.66		●	
Campania Greco	p.68	●		
Santorini Assyrtiko	p.70	●		
Rueda Verdejo	p.72		●	
Hunter Valley Semillon	p.74	●		
Yarra Valley Chardonnay	p.76			●
Hawke's Bay Chardonnay	p.78			
Marlborough Sauvignon Blanc	p.80			●
SPARKLING				
English Sparkling	p.82	●		
Champagne	p.84			●

WHO ARE YOU DINING WITH?

A DATE	FUTURE IN-LAWS	CLIENT	FOODIE OR WINE GEEK	PALS
				•
		•		
•				
				•
			•	
			•	
				•
			•	
				•
	•			
		•		
				•
		•		
			•	
		•		
	•			
			•	
•				
			•	
				•
			•	
•				
	•			
			•	
		•		

WINES		SMALL DINNER PARTY	BIG CASUAL GROUP	ELEGANT COCKTAIL PARTY
SPARKLING (CONTINUED)				
Alsace Crémant	p.86	●		
Veneto Prosecco	p.88		●	
Penedès Cava	p.90		●	
ROSÉ				
Tavel Rosé	p.92			
Provence Bandol Mourvèdre	p.94			
Corsica Patrimonio Nielluccio	p.96	●		
Lombardy Chiaretto	p.98	●	●	
Navarra Rosado	p.100		●	
LIGHT RED				
Willamette Valley Pinot Noir	p.102	●		
Sonoma Coast Pinot Noir	p.104			●
Burgundy Pinot Noir	p.106			●
Beaujolais Gamay	p.108		●	
Loire Cabernet Franc	p.110	●		
Jura Poulsard	p.112	●		
Burgenland Zweigelt	p.114		●	
Central Otago Pinot Noir	p.116	●		
BOLD RED				
Washington Red Blend	p.118	●		
Napa Valley Red Blend	p.120		●	
Sonoma County Zinfandel	p.122		●	
Paso Robles Syrah Blend	p.124			●
Central Valley Carménère	p.126		●	
Mendoza Malbec	p.128		●	
Left-Bank Bordeaux Cab Sauv	p.130			●
Right-Bank Bordeaux Merlot	p.132	●		
Languedoc-Roussillon Red Blend	p.134		●	

A DATE	FUTURE IN-LAWS	CLIENT	FOODIE OR WINE GEEK	PALS
	●			
●				
				●
	●			
		●		
			●	
●				
				●
				●
		●		
		●		
●				
			●	
			●	
				●
	●			
	●			
		●		
●				
●				
	●			
				●
		●		
●				
●				

WINES		SMALL DINNER PARTY	BIG CASUAL GROUP	ELEGANT COCKTAIL PARTY
BOLD RED (CONTINUED)				
Rhône Red Blend	p.136			
Piedmont Barolo	p.138	●		
Valpolicella Amarone	p.140	●		
Alto Adige Lagrein	p.142	●		
Chianti Sangiovese	p.144	●		
Abruzzo Montepulciano	p.146		●	
Puglia Primitivo	p.148	●		
Douro Red Blend	p.150			●
Catalonia Garnacha	p.152			●
Rioja Tempranillo Blend	p.154	●		
Murcia Monastrell	p.156		●	
Western Cape Pinotage	p.158			●
Barossa Valley Shiraz	p.160		●	
Margaret River Cab Sauv	p.162	●		
SWEET & SPIRITED				
Niagara Peninsula Icewine	p.164			●
Loire Chenin Blanc	p.166	●		
Bordeaux Sauternes Sémillon	p.168			●
Cognac Ugni Blanc	p.170			●
Rheingau Riesling	p.172	●		
Tokaj Tokaji Aszú	p.174	●		
Veneto Grappa	p.176		●	
Tuscan Vin Santo	p.178		●	
Douro Port	p.180		●	
Madeira Malmsey	p.182			●
Jerez Sherry	p.184	●		

A DATE	FUTURE IN-LAWS	CLIENT	FOODIE OR WINE GEEK	PALS
		•		
		•	•	
•				
			•	
				•
	•			•
			•	
		•		
				•
	•			
			•	
			•	
				•
	•			
•				
	•			
		•		
		•		
			•	
			•	
				•
				•
		•		
	•			
			•	

WHAT'S COOKING?

WINES		APPETIZERS	SALAD Vinaigrette	Creamy or Caesar	Vegetable	SOUP OR STEW Lentil	Chowder	Mediterranean	FISH OR SHELLFISH Raw	Smoked	Poached	Fried	Grilled
DELICATE WHITE													
Washington Riesling	p.36	•								•			
New York Riesling	p.38	•								•			
Loire Chenin & Sauvignon Blanc	p.40	•								•			
Gascony White Blend	p.42	•	•	•									
Mosel Riesling	p.44									•			
Vaud & Valais Chasselas	p.46	•					•				•		
Friuli Pinot Grigio	p.48	•						•				•	
Marches Verdicchio	p.50			•	•						•		•
Orvieto Trebbiano	p.52	•										•	
Galicia Albariño	p.54						•	•				•	
FULL-BODIED WHITE													
California Chardonnay	p.56						•			•			
Casablanca Sauvignon Blanc	p.58	•							•				
Alsace Riesling	p.60					•							•
Burgundy Chardonnay	p.62						•			•			
Rhône White Blend	p.64					•							
Wachau Grüner Veltliner	p.66		•	•	•								
Campania Greco	p.68			•									
Santorini Assyrtiko	p.70	•	•				•		•			•	•
Rueda Verdejo	p.72	•			•	•	•	•				•	
Hunter Valley Semillon	p.74	•							•		•		
Yarra Valley Chardonnay	p.76						•			•			
Hawke's Bay Chardonnay	p.78						•			•			
Marlborough Sauvignon Blanc	p.80	•							•				
SPARKLING													
English Sparkling	p.82	•									•		
Champagne	p.84	•		•			•				•		

	VEGETABLES						SAUCE					OTHER		MEAT						
	Winter veggies	Spring veggies	Summer veggies	Cauliflower or corn	Dark leafy greens	Green beans, broccoli	Tomato	Herb or cream	Curry	Ginger	Hot chilli peppers	Eggs	Mushroom	Pâté or offal	Beef	Charcuterie	Roasted white meat	Sausages	CHEESE	DESSERT
		●								●	●			●						●
		●										●		●						●
	●	●								●	●									●
				●		●	●													●
	●								●	●	●	●								●
			●		●															●
			●	●	●	●	●													
			●	●	●	●	●													
			●	●		●	●													
			●	●																
				●			●	●					●				●			
		●			●			●												●
	●				●									●						●
				●	●	●		●	●			●					●			
	●				●			●	●				●				●			
		●			●	●				●										
			●				●			●										●
			●				●													●
			●			●														●
										●										
			●					●	●			●					●			
			●	●	●	●		●	●			●					●			
		●				●		●												●
		●																●		●
	●			●								●		●				●		●

WINES		APPETIZERS	SALAD		SOUP OR STEW				FISH OR SHELLFISH				
			Vinaigrette	Creamy or Caesar	Vegetable	Lentil	Chowder	Mediterranean	Raw	Smoked	Poached	Fried	Grilled
SPARKLING (CONTINUED)													
Alsace Crémant	p.86	●			●						●		●
Veneto Prosecco	p.88	●	●						●		●		
Penedès Cava	p.90			●			●			●	●		
ROSÉ													
Tavel Rosé	p.92					●		●		●			
Provence Bandol Mourvèdre	p.94		●	●			●				●		●
Corsica Patrimonio Nielluccio	p.96	●	●	●			●		●		●		
Lombardy Chiaretto	p.98	●	●								●		
Navarra Rosado	p.100					●		●			●		
LIGHT RED													
Willamette Valley Pinot Noir	p.102	●	●										●
Sonoma Coast Pinot Noir	p.104												●
Burgundy Pinot Noir	p.106		●		●	●							●
Beaujolais Gamay	p.108	●	●		●	●							●
Loire Cabernet Franc	p.110	●			●	●							●
Jura Poulsard	p.112	●							●				●
Burgenland Zweigelt	p.114					●				●			
Central Otago Pinot Noir	p.116				●	●							●
BOLD RED													
Washington Red Blend	p.118												
Napa Valley Red Blend	p.120												
Sonoma County Zinfandel	p.122												
Paso Robles Syrah Blend	p.124												
Central Valley Carménère	p.126				●	●							
Mendoza Malbec	p.128												
Left-Bank Bordeaux Cab Sauv	p.130					●							
Right-Bank Bordeaux Merlot	p.132					●							

	VEGETABLES						SAUCE					OTHER			MEAT					
	Winter veggies	Spring veggies	Summer veggies	Cauliflower or corn	Dark leafy greens	Green beans, broccoli	Tomato	Herb or cream	Curry	Ginger	Hot chilli peppers	Eggs	Mushroom	Pâté or offal	Beef	Charcuterie	Roasted white meat	Sausages	CHEESE	DESSERT
		•															•			•
		•	•														•			•
				•		•						•		•			•			•
	•		•		•	•	•									•	•			
		•	•		•	•		•					•				•			
		•	•		•	•							•				•			•
		•	•																	
		•			•		•									•	•			
	•	•		•	•							•					•			
	•	•	•	•	•							•					•			
	•	•	•	•	•							•					•			
	•	•		•	•							•			•		•	•		•
	•			•	•							•		•	•	•		•		
		•		•	•							•		•	•	•	•	•		•
	•	•		•	•							•		•	•	•	•			
	•	•	•	•	•							•					•			
	•			•	•				•		•	•			•		•			•
	•	•							•		•	•			•		•			
	•								•	•	•			•	•	•	•			•
	•			•	•		•		•	•	•	•			•					
	•						•		•	•		•			•		•			•
	•								•	•			•		•					
	•								•	•			•		•					
	•		•								•	•			•	•				

WINES

	APPETIZERS	Vinaigrette	Creamy or Caesar	Vegetable	Lentil	Chowder	Mediterranean	Raw	Smoked	Poached	Fried	Grilled
BOLD RED (CONTINUED)												
Languedoc-Roussillon Red Blend p.134					•							•
Rhône Red Blend p.136					•							
Piedmont Barolo p.138					•							
Valpolicella Amarone p.140												
Alto Adige Lagrein p.142				•	•							
Chianti Sangiovese p.144				•								
Abruzzo Montepulciano p.146							•					
Puglia Primitivo p.148					•							
Douro Red Blend p.150					•							
Catalonia Garnacha p.152							•					
Rioja Tempranillo Blend p.154					•					•		•
Murcia Monastrell p.156					•							
Western Cape Pinotage p.158				•	•			•	•			
Barossa Valley Shiraz p.160												
Margaret River Cab Sauv p.162					•							
SWEET & SPIRITED												
Niagara Peninsula Icewine p.164												
Loire Chenin Blanc p.166												
Bordeaux Sauternes Sémillon p.168												
Cognac Ugni Blanc p.170												
Rheingau Riesling p.172												
Tokaj Tokaji Aszú p.174												
Veneto Grappa p.176								•				
Tuscan Vin Santo p.178												
Douro Port p.180												
Madeira Malmsey p.182					•			•				
Jerez Sherry p.184	•	•	•	•	•	•	•	•	•	•	•	•

	VEGETABLES						SAUCE					OTHER			MEAT					
	Winter veggies	Spring veggies	Summer veggies	Cauliflower or corn	Dark leafy greens	Green beans, broccoli	Tomato	Herb or cream	Curry	Ginger	Hot chilli peppers	Eggs	Mushroom	Pâté or offal	Beef	Charcuterie	Roasted white meat	Sausages	CHEESE	DESSERT
	●		●	●	●		●						●		●	●	●	●	●	
	●		●	●	●						●		●		●		●	●		
	●								●	●			●		●					
													●		●					
	●		●	●	●		●								●	●	●	●		
	●		●	●	●		●						●		●	●	●	●	●	
	●		●	●	●		●						●		●	●	●	●	●	
	●						●						●		●	●				
	●		●	●	●								●		●	●	●	●		
	●		●				●		●		●		●		●	●	●	●		
	●		●	●	●								●		●	●	●	●		
	●		●		●		●						●		●	●	●			
	●		●		●		●						●		●	●				
	●								●	●	●				●					
	●					●			●		●	●			●					
									●	●	●									●
									●	●	●			●						●
														●					●	●
														●					●	●
									●	●	●								●	●
														●					●	●
																				●
																			●	●
																●	●		●	●
												●								●
			●	●	●	●	●		●	●					●		●		●	●

Chapter Three

EXPLORE THE WORLD OF WINE

Now for the wines. This chapter features seventy-five of them and mentions scores more. They're ordered by style, not region, since most of us aren't walking wine atlases. There are also pronunciations, because how useful is it to know everything about Viognier if you don't even know how to say it? And there are mnemonic descriptors (highlighted in bold) to help you commit the information to memory, if you decide to give it a shot.

WASHINGTON RIESLING

From the east, Washington State looks like a perfectly nice rectangle. From the west, it looks like it has been attacked by rabid ravens for no reason. In the middle, the state's most prolific Riesling vineyards follow a north-west-leaning line from the Tri-Cities to Wenatchee.

UNITED STATES

WASHINGTON

WENATCHEE

TRI-CITIES

TOP TERMS

Riesling *(REEZ-ling)*: Cold winters and sunny summers make for Rieslings fragrant with white flowers and ripe apricots. These wines are, for the most part, so inexpensive that you will be *feeling* like you are *stealing*.
Dry/Sweet: The back labels on most bottles of Washington Riesling helpfully indicate whether the wine is Dry, Medium Dry, Medium Sweet, or Sweet. But don't be put off by the middle of the spectrum, as a touch of sweetness is the ideal foil for food.

GEO QUIZ

Columbia Valley/Yakima *(YAAK-ih-MAH)* **Valley**: While the west side of the Cascade Mountain range is damp and heavily forested, the east side is a collection of *valleys* that get so *cold* in the winter that you'll wish you had a *collie's coat*. Summers can be as hot as a *yellow jacket's* sting.
Horse Heaven Hills (HHH)/Ancient Lakes: When *ancient horses die and go to heaven*, it's surely a verdant place with *hills and lakes*. HHH is a Columbia Valley

Looks like the Bavarian Alps, feels like Washington

sub-zone that's nearly as large as the Yakima Valley; it follows the Columbia River to the point where the river bends to the north. Closer to Canada, Ancient Lakes sits on the banks of the Columbia as it runs north to south. It's surrounded by—wouldn't you know it—lakes.

LANDMARK

Leavenworth, Washington, is the next-best thing to a trip to Germany. The Okanagan-Wenatchee Forest could pass for the Black Forest and the Cascade Mountains could stand in for the Bavarian Alps. So have dinner in one of the half-timbered restaurants here, and be sure to order the local Riesling for the full immersive experience.

DON'T STOP THERE

Sauvignon Blanc *(SOH-vin-YOH blahnk)*: Washington does big business in Bordeaux grape varieties, and Sauvignon Blanc is one of them. Unlike the *sour* Sauvignon you might be used to, Washington Sauv Blanc gets quite ripe during the *sunblock*-slathered summers, taking on notes of pineapple and honey. It's often aged in oak, in the Bordeaux style.

Sémillon *(seh-mee-YOH)*: This other Bordeaux white grape isn't as prevalent in Washington, but it makes a medium-to-hearty white wine here, with notes of toasted nuts and ripe *melon* that would pair nicely with *salmon*.

GORGE-OUS GEWURZ

Gewürztraminer *(gay-VOORS-trah-MEEN-er)* is a pink-skinned grape that, at its best, makes a silky white wine that smells like lychee fruit and rose petals. At *its worst,* it's stinky, **lean on flavor**, hot with alcohol, and excessively unctuous. It needs sun to ripen, but can get flabby if it doesn't retain its acidity. The windblown, sun-beaten cliff-top vineyards of the western end of the Columbia Gorge are among the rare places that do this spicy grape justice. But this Washington/Oregon border region changes dramatically as it moves inland from the Pacific Ocean. While Germanic Gewürztraminer (Germany uses the ü) works in the west, the arid eastern stretch of this wine region favors sun-loving grapes like Zinfandel.

NEW YORK RIESLING

New York's viticultural areas are scattered from Lake Erie and Niagara Escarpment to Long Island, the arm that reaches out from New York City with an open hand. North of the big city, grapes grow in bucolic Hudson River Valley. And the center of the action is at the center of the state, around Finger Lakes.

UNITED STATES

NEW YORK

FINGER LAKES

TOP TERMS

Riesling (*REEZ-ling*): Riesling, as ***reinterpreted*** by New York vintners, ranges from dry to off-dry to rich and sweet, typically with low alcohol levels and ***reeking*** (deliciously) of ripe peaches, often with a silky texture and a hint of spritz.

Finger Lakes: These long, thin, ***finger-like*** lakes are between and below the cities of Rochester and Syracuse. The moderating effect of the water staves off spring freezes and softens searing summer heat, making delicate whites that pair deliciously with elegant ***finger*** food.

GEO QUIZ

Niagara Escarpment: This bridge between Lake Erie and Lake Ontario is where New York state meets Canada's Niagara Peninsula—which has its own "Niagara Escarpment" appellation, just to confuse all of us. Whichever side of ***Niagara Falls*** your ***car is parked on***, you're well positioned to grow Riesling grapes.

CULTURAL SNAPSHOT

New Yorkers love their winemakers and their cheesemongers. (There's even a cheese museum in a town called Rome.) Visitors to the Finger Lakes get the best of both, because this wine region is also awash in creameries.

The Finger Lakes are renowned for their numerous waterfalls

LANDMARK

At Taughannock *(tuh-GAA-nuk)* Falls State Park, a 400-foot (122-meter) deep ravine culminates in a waterfall that's 33 feet (10 meters) taller than Niagara Falls. The gorge reveals the richness of this region from a viticultural perspective, exposing layers of sandstone, shale, and limestone. After taking in the views, walk to the shore of Cayuga Lake, where a swim in the clear, icy-cold water is as refreshing as a glass of Riesling.

DON'T STOP THERE

Lake Erie, Ohio: Lake Erie, New York, has historically grown gobs of Concord, a red grape that isn't for fine winemaking (it's described as smelling "foxy," which sounds somewhat *eerie*), but is used to make kosher wines and jellies. However, growers in the Ohio section of this cross-border appellation are beginning to make inroads with Riesling.

Old Mission Peninsula, Michigan: If you're on a *mission* to find the best up-and-coming Riesling regions, check the finger of land that sticks straight up out of Traverse City into *Lake Michigan*.

Willamette *(wil-AM-it)* Valley, Oregon: All the way over on the west coast, Washington State gets all the Riesling glory. But Oregon also produces fresh, delicate, *dynamic* and often *organic* cool-climate Riesling.

LOIRE CHENIN & SAUVIGNON BLANC

Viewed from the top, the Loire River looks like a seagull in flight. The Loire Valley wine region follows its path, from Pouilly-sur-Loire, a couple hours south of Paris, all the way to the west coast, where white-feathered seagulls are a dime a dozen.

LOIRE

FRANCE

TOP TERMS

Vouvray *(VOO-vray)*: Like the most frequently **viewed play** in the world, everyone has opinions about it even if they haven't seen, er, tasted it. No, Chenin Blanc from Vouvray is not necessarily sweet, despite what you may have heard.
Sancerre *(SAHN-sair)*: Vibrant, grassy Sancerre Sauv Blanc is such a perfect match for fresh spring produce and summer salads that you'll be reaching for your **sandals** the moment you taste it.

KEY PLAYERS

Chenin Blanc *(SHUH-nuh BLAH)*: This fragrant white grape can be made into a diverse array of white wines, from bone-dry to sweet to sparkling. Texture-wise, it can range from weightless as **shaving cream** to unctuous as **shea butter**.
Sauvignon Blanc *(SOH-vin-YOH BLAH)*: While New Zealand and Chile make Sauv Blanc that smells **soapy** white, like Irish Spring, Loire Valley Sauv Blanc is more subtle and **savory**.

CULTURAL SNAPSHOT

The west coast of France is famous for its fresh oysters and the Loire Valley is famous for its oyster-friendly white wines. Muscadet is an oft-cited match, but any dry Loire white will complement this briny treat.

It's always a party at an open-air guinguette on the Loire River

LANDMARK

If you're strolling along the Loire River during the summer months, you'll soon stumble across a riverside café decorated with festive strings of lights. These open-air gathering spots, called *guinguettes*, specialize in fresh local fish and live music. You can sip crisp Loire whites all the way through your meal, especially if you finish with a local *chèvre*.

DIGGING DEEPER

Montlouis (*MOHN-lwee*): Just across the river from Vouvray but less well-known, Montlouis also practices *monogamy*, never straying from Chenin Blanc.

Savennières (*SAA-ven-YAIR*): A highly regarded village, known for dry Chenin Blanc that can easily be cellared for longer than *seven years*.

Pouilly-Fumé (*poo-YEE foo-MAY*): Don't worry, the *fumes* from this Sauvignon Blanc (from the tip of the seagull's eastern wing) aren't even remotely *poo-y*. These wines can be weighty but subtle, with notes of citrus and minerality.

EXTRA CREDIT

MEET MUSCADET

Muscadet (*MOOS-kah-DAY*): The *three musketeers* of Loire white grapes are Chenin Blanc, Sauvignon Blanc and the otherwise-rare Melon de Bourgogne. It grows in Muscadet, the area around Nantes where the Loire feeds into the Atlantic Ocean. And it's the ideal match for salt-water *mollusks*, such as *mussels*.

Muscadet-Sèvre-et Main (*MOOS-kah-DAY SEV-ray-MAN*): Most Muscadet labels bear the name of this, the largest sub-appellation. These delicious, sea-foamy wines are underpriced, making them affordable for *every man*.

Sur Lie (*SYOOR LEE*): If the label indicates that it has aged—on the lees—or macerated with the *pearly debris* that falls to the bottom of the barrel, the Muscadet will have a slightly yeasty flavor and creamy texture.

GASCONY WHITE BLEND

The Sud-Ouest (SOOD west) *is a massive blob of land, bordering Spain and the Atlantic Ocean, producing everything from devilishly dark reds to Armagnac. The award for highest productivity goes to the Côtes de Gascogne (KOHT duh GAHS-koh-nyuh), aka Gascony, for its sea of approachable white wines.*

FRANCE

GASCONY

TOP TERMS

Ugni Blanc *(UH-nyee BLAH)*: Surprise! You probably never heard of France's most-planted grape until now. Because this **ugly blonde**, mildly herbaceous and apple-y, is nearly always blended with something else to increase its attractiveness. It's called Trebbiano in Italy.

Colombard *(KOH-lohm-bahr)*: Like the **columns and bars** that hold a building together, Colombard is reliable and sturdy. When it isn't going into Cognac and Armagnac, this heat-loving grape makes a subtle white wine with notes of grapefruit pith and papaya.

GEO QUIZ

Côtes de Gascogne: Gascony is a vacation destination for tourists interested in **gastronomy**. And its unfussy white country wines are staples at restaurants all over the world, where they're often dubbed the "House White."

Saint Mont *(SAHN mohn)*: The sub-zone of Saint Mont in southwestern Gascony is best-known for its robust

CULTURAL SNAPSHOT

D'Artagnan, seventeenth-century spy and Musketeer from Gascony, would have appreciated a light, refreshing white after a sweaty day of dueling, escaping, swashbuckling, and eating Gascony's fatty foie gras and rich cheeses.

In Gascony, every day is market day

reds. Its minerally, citrusy whites (and rosés) occupy a higher spot on the quality *mountain* than your basic Côtes de Gascogne *sandwich* wine.

LANDMARK

In Europe, open-air markets are a dime a dozen. Then there is the true farmers market, run by farmers, that's a rural town's gathering place and grocery store, offering fresh produce, flowers, and meat. In gastronomic Gascony, you'll also find duck confit, pâté, large stinky wheels of cheese, wild mushrooms, and even live animals for those who won't compromise on freshness.

DIGGING DEEPER

Gaillac *(GUY-yak)*: East of Gascony, there's this *guy* who makes enough white styles—dry to sweet to sparkling—to make you *yak* if you were to drink them all at once. The pear-scented native Mauzac *(MOH-zak)* grape rules here; the higher-elevation Première Côtes is a quality sub-zone.

Charentais *(SHAH-rahn-TAY)*: Armagnac distillers get first dibs on the white grapes of Gascony, and the same thing is true in Cognac, to the north. It's not a *charade,* but because they aren't exactly grown for the way they *taste* as dry whites, Charentais wines are inexpensive, just like Gascony whites are.

MOSEL RIESLING

The national mascot on the coat of arms of Germany, a black eagle with wings outstretched, echoes the geographic shape of the nation. The Mosel (MOH-zul) Valley is a feather in the eagle's west wing, following the winding path of the Mosel River from the western Luxembourg border east to the river's intersection with the Rhine.

GERMANY

MOSEL

Joh. Jos. Prüm

Riesling
Kabinett

TOP TERMS

Prädikat *(preh-dee-KAHT)*: Keeping track of all the different ripeness levels of German Riesling is a task on par with convincing six felines to walk in a single-file line *(a parade of cats)*. Still, getting a grip on the Prädikat system is a must.

Riesling *(REEZ-ling)*: Germany's top grape makes a breezy, weightless, dry wine, with piercing acidity and food-friendly accents of citrus and apples. It's like **Reese Witherspoon** in *Wild*—surprisingly raw and transparent.

DIGGING DEEPER

Kabinett *(KAA-bee-NEHT)*: The lightest style of fine German Riesling, made from grapes picked at the least-ripe stage, is light-bodied and fragrant. Imagine Reese, in the **cabin** of an airplane, looking out the window at light, fluffy clouds.

Spätlese *(SHPATE-lay-zuh)*: Made from riper grapes, a fuller-bodied, fruitier Riesling that's still crisp with acidity and **slate** notes. Now Reese is in a **space station**.

CULTURAL SNAPSHOT

The Buddha Museum might look out of place on the Mosel riverfront. But German Riesling has an affinity with cuisines of Buddhist cultures. Try a Kabinett with sushi or a Thai salad roll; Spätlese with *banh mi*; or Auslese with Indian masala.

Bremmer Calmont is one of the world's steepest vineyards

Auslese *(OWS-lay-zuh)*: Rich, viscous, and made from ultra-ripe grapes. Reese is in *outer space* now: far out.

LANDMARK

At a hairpin turn in the Mosel, Bremmer Calmont vineyard nearly qualifies as a cliff. For centuries, intrepid vinetenders have climbed steps set in perilous terrace walls, determined to exploit the intense sunlight that the 65° angle affords. The soil brims with chunks of slate, reflecting light and heat on the grapevines

DIGGING EVEN DEEPER

Trocken *(TRAHK-un)*: A term that indicates the wine is dry, and will be zippy with acidity. Think of zipping along a hard, dry highway, on which the tires of your truck get terrific *traction*.

Halbtrocken *(HALB-TRAHK-un)*: These are medium-dry Rieslings, perhaps a bit softer, like a road after a snowstorm in which you only get *half traction* (and there's a dusting of powdered sugar on everything.) Confusingly, Spätleses are not always *halbtrocken*.

Feinherb *(FINE-hairb)*: Sweet. Turn a bunch of bees loose in a field of *fine herbs* and wildflowers and they will make a fragrant honey, similar in aroma and flavor to a *feinherb* Auslese. And, of course, your truck wouldn't get any traction on a honey-covered road.

EXTRA CREDIT

LABEL TERMS TO KNOW

Erste Lage *(AIR-stay LAH-guh)*: Like the French term Premier Cru, this denotes that the grapes were grown in one of the second-best vineyards in Germany. There are ordinary lumberjacks and then there are *hirsute loggers*, those big hairy guys who don't even need a chainsaw—they can chop down a tree with an old-fashioned axe.

Grosse Lage *(GROH-suh LAH-guh)*: The German word for the top vineyards in the nation, it's the equivalent of Grand Cru. It isn't just any *logger*, but one of the world's best loggers. He weighs a *gross* and makes a fantastic *gross profit*.

Grosses Gewächs *(GROH-sus geh-VAAKS)* or just **GG**: This term appears on the labels of *trocken*, or bone-dry, wines sourced from Grosse Lage vineyards. That *logger* who weighs a *gross can whack* down a tree without even breaking a sweat—he stays dry.

VAUD & VALAIS CHASSELAS

The little-known wine regions of Switzerland beckon to the rest of the world with their alluring whites. Prestigious Vaud curves like a shoulder over Lake Geneva (Lac Léman) from the city of Geneva. To its west, prolific Valais reaches out to pull Italy's leg.

TOP TERMS

Chasselas *(SHAH-say-LAHSS)*: This white Swiss grape also goes by "Fendant" and "Perlan," just to keep us on our toes. It's best when vinified as a drink-now wine that's as weightless as **dental floss**, and soft and silky as your **cat's** sleek coat. The Swiss say it smells like Linden trees; think smoky, citrusy, and creamy.

Müller-Thurgau *(MOOH-ler TUHR-gow)*: Although it's more prevalent in Germany, the Müller-Thurgau grape was born in the Swiss canton of Thurgau. It makes a weightless peachy wine with notes of **mulled cider**.

DIGGING DEEPER

Lavaux *(lah-VOH)*/**Dézaley** *(DAY-zah-LAY)*/**Calamin** *(KAH-lah-MEEN)*: In the Lavaux sub-region of Vaud, the world's finest Grand Cru Chasselas vineyards get wine-lovers worked into a **lather**. Dézaley and neighboring Calamin, overlooking Lake Geneva, are so **dizzyingly** steep that they'll cause your heart to race; a spot of **chamomile** tea is a good way to calm down.

CULTURAL SNAPSHOT

Raclette is basically five-minute fondue. It's prepared by heating a half-wheel of Swiss mountain cheese. Holding the waxy shell, the server scrapes the gooey molten middle onto your plate. Wash it down with a glass of Chasselas.

Yodeling is entirely appropriate in the vineyards of the Lavaux sub-zone, Vaud

Petite Arvine *(peh-TEET ahr-VEEN)*: The world supply of this grape would fit in a few *small RVs*. It makes a textured white, with crisp acidity and notes of grapefruit; it is also made into a late-harvest dessert wine.

LANDMARK

The terraced vineyards of Vaud and Valais can be so precipitously steep that some are outfitted with tiny gondolas or funicular systems to transport heavy loads of grapes and equipment back down to earth level. So when skiers ride the cable car to the glacier atop nearby mountain Les Diablerets, they're acting like a bunch of grapes.

GEO QUIZ

Neuchâtel *(NOO-shah-TELL)*: In the "Three Lakes" area—just north of Vaud and Valais, between the banks of Lac de Neuchâtel and the French border—Neuchâtel is another prominent Swiss wine region noted for its Chasselas. Is it a good match for *Neufchâtel* cheese? Well, of course it is!

Valle d'Aosta *(VAH-lay dah-OH-stah)*: Forgive the *delay* while I *stray* to a northwestern Italian region that's like a sister to Switzerland. The *postal* codes might differ, but the two share a love for Petite Arvine, Müller-Thurgau, Pinot Noir, and Gamay, as well as the rare Prié Blanc.

FRIULI PINOT GRIGIO

Fine-grained Slavonian oak from Croatia is a popular wine barrel material, so it's fitting that Friuli-Venezia Giulia (free-OO-lee ven-ETS-ee-ah JOOL-ee-ah), the Italian wine region that's a stone's throw from Croatia, should be shaped like an oak leaf. This is white wine country, so maybe think of a white oak when you think of Friuli.

FRIULI-VENEZIA GIULIA

ITALY

TOP TERMS

Pinot Grigio *(PEE-noh GREE-joh)*: *Peevish* northeastern Italian winemakers would like to *peel off* Pinot Grigio's *egregious* reputation as a boring wine.

Friuli Colli Orientali *(free-OO-lee KOH-lee OH-ree-en-TAHL-ee)*: Important sub-region of Friuli, noted for its crackling complex whites. Bottles labeled "Sauvignon," for example, will force you to *collate* and *re-orient* your preconception of Sauvignon Blanc. Prepare for luscious tropical *fruit* flavors interspersed with fresh herb accents.

DIGGING DEEPER

Friulano *(FREE-ooh-LAH-noh)*: The namesake white grape of Friuli is a close relative of Sauvignon Blanc and at its best can taste *fruity*, like pears and peaches, with a pecan-walnut finish.

Pinot Bianco *(PEE-noh bee-YAHN-koh)*: Pinot Grigio has grayish pink—*grigio*—skins. Cousin Pinot Bianco has *whitish*—*bianco*—green skins. It tends toward notes of almond, citrus rind, and sea brine.

CULTURAL SNAPSHOT

Friuli-Venezia Giulia, along with the Veneto and Trentino-Alto Adige, make up the Tre Venezie (or Triveneto). Bordering Austria, Slovenia, and Croatia, it can feel like a foreign country to travelers from central or southern Italy.

Friuli's whites are like Sella Nevea's slopes: brisk and brimming with minerality

LANDMARK

Bracing acidity and intense minerality are trademarks of Friulian white wines, thanks to the region's position in the foothills of the Carnic and Julian Alps, where the soil is rocky and the high-elevation breezes are cool. At Sella Nevea ski resort, the snow is just as crisp and invigorating. The peak affords commanding views of the jagged surrounding mountains; from here, skiers can bomb down the backside across the Slovenian border, then ride a chairlift back to Italy.

DON'T STOP

Soave *(SWAH-vay)*: The white wine of the Veneto region is typically crisp and simple. The best producers, however, make rich, full-bodied Soaves that are spicy, smoky, and luxuriant. *Suave*, in fact.

Garganega *(GAHR-gah-NAY-gah)*: The predominant white grape of the Soave region and its namesake wine grows in *gargantuan* loose bunches. Higher-quality vineyards prune fruit from each vine to ensure more even and complete ripening.

Classico/Superiore *(KLAHSS-ee-koh/soo-PAIR-ee-OH-ray)*: One or both of these words on a Soave label indicate that the grapes came from the *classic*, traditional Soave-growing zone in the hills (as opposed to the flats). Here, small family wineries craft *superior* Soave.

ORANGE WINE

So-called orange, or amber, wines, are made from traditional white wine grapes that have been allowed to macerate in open-air vats. As is typical in red winemaking, the juice soaks up color, tannin, and texture from the skins. (White winemaking more commonly calls for squeezing the juice off the skins and siphoning it into airtight tanks for freshness.) Pinot Grigio grapes are well-suited to this style because their skins have a russet hue to them, making for a wine that ranges in color from *orange* to watermelon.

Ribolla *(ree-BOH-lah)*: A white grape common to Friuli and Slovenia (where it is spelled Rebula). It is a favorite among the *rebellious* winemakers who prefer to produce it as an orange wine.

MARCHES VERDICCHIO

Weight-lifting champions have torsos that look like the letter "V." And the torso of Italy specializes in white wine grapes with names that start with the letter "V." Coincidence? I think not. Verdicchio rules in the Marches, or Marche (MARH-kay) in Italian, the central coastal region that's due east of Tuscany. Vernaccia and Vermentino both call Tuscany home.

MARCHES

ITALY

TOP TERMS

Verdicchio *(vair-DEEK-yoh)*: This grape makes a dry white that smells like a *verdant* garden. The *key* to pairing it? Stick to herbaceous foods like pesto, rosemary chicken, or fish poached with tarragon. Pleasantly tart on the palate, Verdicchio ranges in texture and it can even make a crisp and zesty sparkling wine.

Castelli di Jesi *(kahss-TELL-ee dee YEZ-ee)*: Sadly, you will not be absolved of your sins by drinking Verdicchio from its best-known zone in the Marches because the *castles* don't belong to *Jesus*, but rather to the unassuming fortified town of Jesi, around which there are some very nice vineyards.

DIGGING DEEPER

Vernaccia *(vair-NAH-chah)*: Affordable, pleasant, herbaceous and almondy, Vernaccia is Italy's everyday *"vernacular"* white wine (and grape). Its *natural* home is San Gimignano, a town at the west end of Chianti country in Tuscany.

CULTURAL SNAPSHOT

In the early 1950s, Marches wineries commissioned an amphora-shaped Verdicchio bottle to commemorate Ancona's importance as an ancient Greek port. Dubbed "La Lollobrigida," it looked more like the famous actress's figure.

The promontory of Monte Conero, in the Marches

Vermentino *(VAIR-men-TEE-noh)*: A *veritable* approximation of sea foam, seaweed, and hunks of fresh herbs all churned up together in a blender, Vermentino is a shoo-in with Tuscan-style seafood such as grilled shrimp (which are known in some circles as the *vermin of the sea*).

LANDMARK

"Terroir" describes the way a wine can call to mind the place where the grapes were grown. Monte Conero, just south of Ancona in the Marches, flips this concept on its head as it actually looks and smells like a good glass of Verdicchio. Swathed in trees and shrubbery, it's balmy with fresh scents of pine trees, juniper bushes, oleander blossoms, and the salty sand below. A promontory of green in a sea of green, the mountain protrudes into the Adriatic like a capital "V" tipped on its side.

DON'T STOP

Pecorino *(PEHK-oh-REE-noh)*: In the Marches and neighboring region Abruzzo, Pecorino makes a dry white wine that's simple, fruity, and floral. If its name is making you *peckish*, you're thinking about *Pecorino*, the sheep's milk cheese. Apparently Pecorino grape bunches are shaped like the head of a sheep—that's *pecora* in Italian.

ORVIETO TREBBIANO

The well-known name of Orvieto is shared between two regions. Lazio (LAHT-zee-oh), also known as Latium (LAHT-ee-oom), is the knee of the booted leg that is Italy and home to the bustling capital city of Rome. Umbria (OOM-bree-ah) is the dead-center of the nation. Lacking a coastline or a border, it likes to be called "the green heart of Italy."

ITALY
UMBRIA
LAZIO

TOP TERMS

Orvieto *(ohr-vee-EHT-oh)*: This region is **oriented** around the Umbrian city of the same name. Most of today's Orvieto whites, made from a blend of grapes, are *secco* (dry), although a sweeter style predominated in centuries past. Basic Orvieto table wines can be a bore, but the best are layered with flavors of hazelnut and **orange**.

Trebbiano *(treh-bee-AH-noh)*: The most-planted grape variety in Italy and the predominant grape in Orvieto, Trebbiano is something of a blank slate by itself, but plays a **treble** high note when blended with rich Malvasia or pungent Grechetto.

DIGGING DEEPER

Classico/Superiore *(KLAH-see-koh/soo-PAIR-ee-OH-ray)*: The **classic** wine-growing area at the center of Orvieto is home to the best vineyard sites. Vines that have been pruned back make richer, more mouthfilling wines of **superior** quality and are labeled as such.

Grechetto *(greh-KAY-toh)*: A rich and powerful blending

CULTURAL SNAPSHOT

The intricate Gothic façade of the Duomo di Orvieto features bas-relief scenes surrounded by frames of grapevines, complete with tiny clusters of fruit. They're as intricate—and rare—as a glass of sweet Orvieto.

Orvieto is naturally fortified by cliffs of tufa, a volcanic ash rock

partner for lightweight Trebbiano in Orvieto. Ripe pears, lime pith, pineapple, and *Greek* baklava-like notes of almonds and honey are typical tasting notes.

Malvasia *(MAHL-vah-ZEE-ah)*: Like *Madonna, or Lady Gaga*, Malvasia shows up everywhere, and always with a different look. It's white (*bianca*), black (*nera*) and everything in between and goes by a gazillion different names. It's also blended with Trebbiano in Orvieto.

LANDMARK

Orvieto was a sacred place for the Etruscans, the pre-Roman people who introduced winemaking to France. In Orvieto they used the local tufa, a volcanic ash rock, to build tombs, underground tunnels, and city walls, as the material was celebrated for its pliable yet strong properties. Vinetenders will tell you that tufa is the secret to the distinct minerality of the region's wines, as well.

GEO QUIZ

Frascati *(frah-SKAH-tee)*: Roman aristocrats used to head to the hills southeast of Rome to cool off, and many of their palatial summer vacation villas (imagine the cost of a *fractional ownership*!) are in Frascati. Surrounded by vineyards, this town's namesake Mal/Treb blends are a staple on Roman wine lists.

GALICIA ALBARIÑO

"Green Spain" is a loose term for the verdant northwestern corner of Spain where green-skinned white wine grapes flourish. It's shaped like a tree lying on its side. The state of Galicia (gah-LEES-ee-ah) is the top of the tree, and the key sub-zone of Rías Baixas (REE-ahss BYE-shahss) looks like a scattering of leaves.

GALICIA

SPAIN

TOP TERMS

Rías Baixas: The most famous white wine sub-region of Galicia. It's composed of five petite, puddle-shaped sub-zones arranged around deep fjord-like inlets that cannot be **bypassed**. Bring your fishing **reel** because seafood abounds in these waters.

Albariño *(AL-bah-REE-nyoh)*: The thick skins of the Albariño grape ward off Galicia's interminable drizzle. Its **albatross** is that it makes two different wines. Vinified in steel tanks, it makes a gauzy aperitif. Aged in barrels, it's slick and higher in alcohol. Either way, its **primo** acidity makes for a vibrant white wine.

DIGGING DEEPER

Valdeorras *(val-DEH-oh-RAHSS)*: Inland, on Galicia's eastern border, Valdeorras is making a **valiant** effort to bring glory to the Godello grape—and it has achieved **success**. Neighboring Ribeira Sacra, Bierzo, and Monterrei also produce good Godello.

Godello *(goh-DEHL-oh)*: If you're looking for a Galician

CULTURAL SNAPSHOT

The scallop shell is the symbol of the Christian pilgrimage route that ends in Galicia at Santiago de Compostela. The plump local Vieira from the Galician coast is considered to be Spain's best scallop. It is, of course, divine alongside Albariño.

Isla de Ons, the perfect place to enjoy a chilled bottle of Albariño

wine with more body and richness, try Godello. This white grape is gaining attention for its smoky minerality. Some wineries are aging it in oak barrels to make a **golden**, Chardonnay-like wine.

LANDMARK

Galicia's Marine National Park consists of small islands at the mouths of the *rías* of the Rías Baixas. Take a ferry to the Isla de Ons to bask on a breezy white-sand beach and witness the nature that abounds in this emerald-green region. Be sure to try the octopus stew (with a glass of Albariño, of course) at one of the island's laid-back restaurants.

DON'T STOP

Minho *(MEE-noh)*: **Minnows** swimming on the northern Spanish side of the Miño River drink Albariño. **Minnows** swimming on the Portuguese side call it the Minho River, and drink Alvarinho.

Vinho Verde *(VEE-noh VAIR-deh)*: The Portuguese wine region of Minho is also, confusingly, called Vinho Verde when the Vinho Verde wine style is being referenced. Spritzy, fragrant, and low in alcohol, this "**green wine**" is typically sold in green bottles. It is a blend of white grapes, often based on Alvarinho, that's released early and should be drunk young.

EXTRA CREDIT

TXAKOLÍ

East of Galicia, Spanish Basque country looks north onto the Bay of Biscay and kisses France's southern border. The climate here favors native grape varieties, each with traditional Basque names—"Hondarribi Zuri," for example—that sound exotic to our ears. This is the land of **Txakoli** *(CHAH-koh-LEE)*, also spelled Chacolí, a low-alcohol, semi-sparkling white (or rosé) that typically comes in green bottles. It tastes like a tart, dry, **chalky** version of Vinho Verde and it's the aperitif of choice in Basque cities like Biarritz, San Sebastián, and Bilbao. The three Txakolí production zones all have the word "Txakolina" in them, so labels might be printed with either word, or both.

CALIFORNIA CHARDONNAY

For most Americans, Cabernet Sauvignon is synonymous with the Napa Valley, but we tend to think of Chardonnay as more generally "Californian." From its sandy beaches to its flaxen deserts and snowy mountaintops, the glistening Golden State is solid gold in its love for Chardonnay.

UNITED STATES

RUSSIAN RIVER VALLEY

SONOMA COAST

NAPA VALLEY

CALIFORNIA

TOP TERMS

Chardonnay *(SHAHR-doh-NAY)*: If you order California Chardonnay, it's **hard to say** what it will taste like. What used to be a monolithic style—smoky oak, marshmallow texture—has now diverged into everything from racy and unoaked wines to smooth and subtle ones.

Carneros *(kahr-NAIR-ohss)*: This cool, foggy region straddles the southern *corners* of both the Napa and Sonoma Valleys, and the Chards reflect both influences.

GEO QUIZ

Russian River Valley/Sonoma Coast: Along the Sonoma Coast shoreline and into the Russian River Valley, maritime breezes and chilly fog make for Chardonnay grapes with frisson. *So no more cussing* about the *Russian-caliber* chill, because it fosters delicious Chardonnay.

Sonoma County: Sonoma County *counts* sixteen sub-appellations within its borders, of which—confusingly—Sonoma Mountain, Sonoma Valley, and Sonoma Coast

CULTURAL SNAPSHOT

California's Gold Rush happened in the Sierra Nevada. Today's gold is digital, and it's being discovered in the Silicon Valley. From certain Santa Cruz Mountains Chard vineyards, you can look down on the tech capital as you sip liquid gold.

Mustard is a useful deterring ground cover in California vineyards

are three. Key Chard sub-zones (in addition to those above) are Alexander Valley, Chalk Hill, and Sonoma Mountain.

LANDMARK

In the eighteenth century, a Franciscan friar hiked from San Diego to Sonoma, establishing missions. He scattered Spanish mustard seeds along the way to create a golden pathway of flowers that he could follow back home. Today, every late winter, California vineyards are carpeted with the pungent plants. You can view the blooms from a scenic trail at Sugarloaf Ridge State Park, which straddles Sonoma and Napa in the Mayacamas Mountains.

DIGGING DEEPER

Central Coast: This stretch between San Francisco and Santa Barbara covers (duh) the *center of the California coast*. Chardonnay hot spots: The Santa Lucia Highlands, a sub-zone of Monterey that's near the city of Soledad; and the Sta Rita Hills, just northwest of Santa Barbara. **Santa Cruz (*KROOZ*) Mountains**: *Cruising* north to south from the Silicon Valley suburb of Woodside to the farming town of Watsonville, this mountainous Central Coast sub-zone gets maritime breezes that make for lively Chardonnays.

CASABLANCA SAUVIGNON BLANC

Like a straw in an ice-filled glass, skinny Chile is chilliest at the bottom, near Antarctica. The wine-growing regions fill the center section, and Sauvignon Blanc country occupies the upper half of this stretch. Can you serve inexpensive Chilean Sauv Blanc in an ice-filled glass? Por qué no?

CASABLANCA

CHILE

TOP TERMS

Casablanca *(KAH-sah-BLAHN-kah)* Valley: Every sub-region in Chile is a "Valley," or "Valle de" in Spanish. Between the bustling cities of Santiago and Valparaíso, coastal Casablanca (which translates as "white house") is like a **greenhouse** for the **white** grape, Sauvignon Blanc.
San Antonio Valley: *San Antonio, Texas*, is south of the White House, and the San Antonio Valley is immediately south of Casablanca. Both coastal sub-zones are inside the larger region of Aconcagua *(AH-kohn-KAH-gwah)*; you might see any of the three names on a Sauv Blanc label.

KEY PLAYERS

Sauvignon Blanc *(SOH-vin-YOH blahnk)*: Lean and minerally in France's Loire Valley, grassy and grapefruity in New Zealand, Sauv Blanc takes on unusually tropical notes of pineapple and passion fruit in Chile. This wine is **so vindicated** when you serve it with *ceviche*.
Chardonnay *(SHAHR-doh-NAY)*: At its simplest, Chilean Chard is a papaya-and-guava-scented pleasure,

CULTURAL SNAPSHOT
This 1873 painting by Chilean artist Manuel Antonio Caro depicts the *cueca*, Chile's national dance. Contrast it with a graceful ballet scene by Degas and you get a sense of the difference between Chilean and Loire Sauvignon Blanc.

Valparaíso is as colorful, inventive, and lively as Chile's wines and cuisine

priced extremely competitively. Higher-end renditions are typically aged in new oak barrels, which bring a **charred**-caramel component to the glass.

LANDMARK

The historic port city of Valparaíso could be the set for a post-apocalyptic film shot in 1940s Technicolor. Colorfully painted nineteenth-century *ascensores*, or funiculars, still transport people up the precipitously steep *ceros*, or hillsides. From the top of any *ascensor*, take in the ocean air and the rainbow-colored jumble of facades that make this town the architectural equivalent of a bag of Skittles, a good tasting note for Chilean Sauvignon Blanc.

GEO QUIZ

Elqui *(EL-kee)* **Valley**: Chile's northernmost wine-growing zone sits on the southern border of the Atacama Desert, where the shade of an **oak tree** would be much appreciated. Elqui Sauv Blanc tends to be citrusy, with exciting accents of chili pepper.

Limarí *(LEE-mah-REE)* **Valley**: Just south of the Elqui Valley, Limarí is cooled (somewhat) by fog off the ocean. It grows a lot of Chardonnay as well as some **limey** Sauvignon Blanc. Both Elqui and Limarí fall within the larger Coquimbo *(koh-KEEM-boh)* region of Chile.

EXTRA CREDIT

CHILE'S LAYER CAKE

Chile's wine-growing appellations are neatly stacked in a column. But within each region, the topography differs dramatically from west to east. Chilean wine aficionados use three terms to distinguish the variety of landscapes. The **Costa (KOH-stah)**, or coastal areas, grow crisp, high-acid fruit. **Entre Cordilleras (EN-tray KOHR-dee-YAIR-ahss)**, the valley between the Coastal Range to the west and the mountains to the east, enjoys reliable weather and makes sturdy wines. And the high-elevation growing areas in the foothills of the **Andes** is so saturated in sunlight that these vineyards grow grapes with concentrated color and flavor. Many of the individual sub-zones—including Limarí—stretch across all three topographies, allowing vintners to blend a balanced wine.

ALSACE RIESLING

Alsace (al-ZASS) is France's eastern shoulder, in the rain shadow of the Vosges Mountains overlooking the Rhine River. It specializes in white wines that are rich, spicy, and surprisingly dry. They're the vinous equivalent of a savory white sauce, which is, incidentally, a delicious match for Alsatian Riesling.

ALSACE

FRANCE

TOP TERMS

Grand Cru *(GRAWN kroo)*: The best vineyards in Alsace- –and the wines are priced accordingly. So don't pour these *grand* wines into your Alsatian-style *fondue*.
Riesling *(REEZ-ling)*: The *breezy* conditions on the hillside vineyards of Alsace render rich, flavorful white wines. *Pleasing* and dry, they're *appeasing* to people who think they "don't like sweet Riesling."

OTHER OPTIONS

Gewurztraminer *(gay-VOORS-trah-meen-er)*: That long, complicated name gives it the *worst demeanor*, but Alsace's second most-important grape makes a lovely low-acid white that's fragrant with notes of lychee, rose petals, and spice (which is *gewürz*, with the ü, in German). It's like a drier, *leaner* version of those spiced rosewater puddings from places like Turkey and India.
Pinot Gris *(PEE-noh GREE)*: The lavender-tinted skins of this white grape explain "*gris*" meaning "*gray*." In Alsace, Pinot Gris tends toward the luscious and baroque.

CULTURAL SNAPSHOT

An Alsatian dog is the same thing as a German Shepherd. Choucroute is the same thing as sauerkraut. But Alsatian Riesling is a much different animal than German Riesling. However, both are delicious with choucroute, or, sauerkraut.

Strasbourg Cathedral: architectural metaphor for Alsatian white wines

It's as if the region's rather simple Pinot Blanc has been ornamented with golden *filigree*.

LANDMARK

The Cathédrale Notre-Dame de Strasbourg (aka Strasbourg Cathedral) was the world's tallest building for more than two hundred and twenty five years and is visible from many northern Alsatian vineyards. Its façade of pink-tinted sandstone, sourced from the Vosges Mountains, matches the pinkish-gold hue of many of Alsace's so-called "white" wines; and its elaborate embellishments make an architectural metaphor for their complexity and opulence.

DIGGING DEEPER

Muscat d'Alsace *(moos-KAHT dal-ZASS)*: This grape makes a dry white that's often oily in texture and fragrant with orange blossoms, apricots, and sometimes a very slight note of something rotten. It works better as a late-harvest dessert wine that tastes like honey-apricot *mousse*.

Gentil *(JAUNT-ee)*: An everyday blend of white grapes is called an Edelzwicker. Fortunately for those of us tasked with finding rhyming words, higher-quality white blend Gentil is more prevalent in good wine shops. It's a more *jaunty, genteel jumble* of white grape varieties.

BURGUNDY CHARDONNAY

Zoom in on a map of Bourgogne (BOOR-GON-yuh), aka Burgundy, and you'll see the profile of a slender person leaning into the wind. And then there's Chablis: 85 miles plus (137 km plus) to the northwest of everything else, it's flying toward Dijon like a piece of debris.

CHABLIS

BURGUNDY

FRANCE

TOP TERMS

Chablis *(SHAB-lee)*: *Chalky* marine sedimentary soils and a dislike for oak barrels make for white wines with a ***seashell*** quality to them. If you're on a budget, check out Petit *(**puh-TEE**)* Chablis, grown in the far suburbs. You'll feel like you're committing ***petty theft*** when you buy a bottle.

Meursault *(MEHR-soh)*: It's said the whites of Meursault can be reminiscent of unctuous bone ***marrow***.

Chardonnay *(SHAHR-doh-NAY)*: If this white grape is sourced from a celebrated vineyard, get out your ***charge card***. If it bears the name of a larger, less-esteemed region like Mâcon, you'll be able to pay cash for it.

LANDMARK

If you were to fly over the town of Auxerre, just west of Chablis on the River L'Yonne, in a plane or helicopter, you'd describe it as red, thanks to all the tile roofs. Even the hulking Gothic Saint-Étienne of Auxerre Cathedral would look like a big red blob. But from street level,

CULTURAL SNAPSHOT

The cream colored town of Chablis could have been carved out of ivory. Even the hillside vineyards seem scored by white lines. Hunks of chalk in the soil make it glisten like a bed of pearls. It goes without saying its famous wines are white.

Auxerre shows its colors

Auxerre is all ivory limestone. Likewise, we tend to think of red Pinot Noir when we think of Burgundy. Chardonnay might play the supporting role, but it can be just as long-lived and monumental.

GEO QUIZ

Côte de Beaune *(KOHT duh bohn)*: The north-central chunk of Burgundy produces mostly blood-red Pinot Noir, but the *bone*-white Chardonnays come from world-famous place names like Meursault. Conveniently, this sub-region surrounds the town of *Beaune* like a *coat*.

Côte Chalonnaise *(KOHT SHAH-loh-nayz)*: Take off your *coat* down in the warm *knees* section of Burgundy, where the wines, like *mayonnaise*, are creamy and shouldn't sit around for long.

Mâcon *(MACK-ohn)*: Burgundy's deep south is a great source for pleasant Chardonnays that *Macklemore* could afford on his thrift-shop budget. Whites labeled **Mâcon Villages** *(vee-LAHZH)* are as charming and uncomplicated as an idyllic country *village*.

Pouilly Fuissé *(poo-YEE FWEE-say)*: The best-known sub-appellation of Mâcon, Pouilly Fuissé turns out rich, flavorful whites that are neither *poo-ey* nor *fussy*. Confusingly, there's an appellation called Pouilly-Fumé in the Loire Valley (see p.41).

(see p.41)

EXTRA CREDIT

ROCKSTAR VINEYARD

Chablis is rich in Grand Cru vineyards, but the top properties in the Côte de Beaune are those known by name all over the globe.

Le Montrachet *(LUH MOH-rah-shay)*: Any Chardonnay with the name Montrachet appended to it (there are lots of hyphenated versions) should be spectacular. But Montrachet alone is like *Morrissey* or *Madonna*—it only goes by one name and once you've had a sample of it, you'll never forget it.

Corton-Charlemagne *(KOHR-tohn SHAHR-leh-MAHN-yuh)*: The emperor *Charlemagne* actually owned the hill of Corton. White wines with either or both names on them are rock stars—in the wine world, anyway—as big as *Kurt Cobain*.

RHÔNE WHITE BLEND

The Northern Rhône follows a lean "l" shape on a map and produces lithe, powerful, pricey whites from just three grape varieties. The warmer southern half of the region is shaped more like an "M" and mixes medleys of many grapes to make magnificently strong, moderately priced white wines.

FRANCE

NORTHERN RHÔNE
SOUTHERN RHÔNE

TOP TERMS

Condrieu *(KOHN-dree-YUH)*: Northern Rhône cru (top vineyard site) famous for—*contrary to* the rest of the region—only one grape, Viognier.

Hermitage *(AIR-mee-TAZH)*: A *hermitage* would be the perfect place to store the Marsanne/Roussanne blends from this famous cru, since they are made for *aging*.

Crôzes-Hermitage *(KROHZ AIR-mee-TAZH)*: *Across* and around *Hermitage*, Crôzes-Hermitage makes the most wine in the Northern Rhône.

KEY PLAYERS

Marsanne *(MAHR-san)*: Like the burly Roman god of war, *Mars*, Marsanne dominates in the Northern Rhône. It makes a powerful, weighty wine.

Roussanne *(ROO-san)*: With its *rosy-tinted* skin and floral aroma, Roussanne accessorizes sturdy Marsanne like a pink *rose in a buttonhole*.

Viognier *(VEE-oh-NYAY)*: Ripe melons and peaches dominate the *bouquet* (aroma) of this fragrant grape.

CULTURAL SNAPSHOT

If Rhône's white grapes were Roman deities, Marsanne would be belligerent *Mars*. Viognier is *Venus*, all peach, nectar, ambrosia. And Roussanne is the garland of *roses* that Venus puts on Mars' head, to soften his image and make him smell better.

The town of Marsanne takes a break from the ravages of the Mistral

LANDMARK

The Rhône River channels a strong wind—called the Mistral—that blows all the way to the Mediterranean Sea. It thickens the skins of grapes, building flavor and tannin; dries out vines, protecting them from rot; and pumps up acidity by cooling the fruit off on hot days.

OTHER OPTIONS

Châteauneuf-du-Pape *(SHAAT-oh-NEHF doo PAHP)*: The Southern Rhône appellation where the *"Pope's new castle"* was built is famous for its reds, and admired for its whites. With their honeycomb aroma, golden color, and velvety texture, they're like a Pope's gilded robes.

Côtes du Rhône Villages Blanc *(KOHT doo ROHN VEE-lahzh BLAH)*: Your basic Côtes du Rhône white is an inexpensive blend based on the Grenache Blanc grape. Go ahead and spring for the higher-level Villages; you won't cry if there's major *spillage*, since they're so affordable.

Grenache Blanc *(GRUH-nash BLAH)*: You might *grimace* upon finding your old white golden retriever snoozing on your bed, *grinning* and drooling on your *blankets*. But Grenache Blanc—the favored grape of the many used in the white blends of the Southern Rhône—is also full-bodied, mellow, and lingering, and it will, eventually, make you grin.

WACHAU GRÜNER VELTLINER

Austria looks like a clam or an oyster, and its name, in German, is Österreich (ih-stir-HIKE). So when you see a word that looks like "oyster rake" on a wine label, think of this oyster-shaped nation and its shellfish-friendly white wine.

WACHAU

AUSTRIA

TOP TERM

Grüner Veltliner *(GROON-ur felt-LEEN-er)*: This white grape *crooned* its way to fame so quickly in the mid-2000s that wine insiders nicknamed it *"groovy"* (get it?). It's more herbaceous and svelte than other full-bodied whites, like Chardonnay or Viognier, and in some cases is light-bodied and fresh, accented by notes of lime pith and grapefruit rind. The more expensive the bottle, the more likely the wine will be plusher (sort of like *felt*), with notes of cream, tropical fruit, ginger, and white pepper.

GEO QUIZ

Niederösterreich *(NEE-dur-ih-stir-HIKE)*: "Nieder" means "lower," but Austria's biggest and most important wine region actually borders the Czech Republic and Slovakia to the *NE* (*northeast*). You might *need an oyster rake* as its key white wine makes a fine pairing with oysters.
Wachau *(vahk-HOW)*: *What cow? That cow.* Niederösterreich's westernmost sub-zone is lush and green, making for happy cows and excellent Grüner.

CULTURAL SNAPSHOT

The Danube River is notable for its green waters and verdant banks. Wachau "Grüner"—German for "greener"—Veltliner comes in a decidedly green bottle. Within the context of fuller-bodied whites, Grüner is *greener* and *leaner* than its peers.

LANDMARK

Vineyards aren't merely the provenance of the countryside. The German name for the city of Vienna is "Wien," so it's fitting that metropolitan Vienna should be an official wine-growing appellation within the Niederösterreich region. Tourists tired of the gorgeous palaces and museums of this historic city can walk the official Vienna Wine Trail, take in the urban vineyard scenery, and make pit stops at *heurige* wine taverns. Bellevuestrasse, which translates as "pretty view street," makes a convenient-to-remember stop for viewing the scenery.

Not all vineyards are rural

DIGGING DEEPER

Kamptal *(kump-TOWL)* and Kremstal *(KREHM-stahl)*: These neighbors of Wachau within the boundaries of Niederösterreich also specialize in groovy Grüner. A *cup* of refreshing Kamptal Grüner feels like *jumping* into the Kamp River (don't forget your *towel*). You might have to nosh on *crème* caramel in a shower *stall* to counteract the spiciness of Grüner from Kremstal.

The long, green Danube River winds though the land of Grüner wine

CAMPANIA GRECO

The shinbone of the Italian boot is home to archaeological sites like Pompeii and Herculaneum. Its finest wines are vinified from archaic grape varieties that would be familiar to ancient Pompeiians. Nearly two thousand years after the eruption of Mt. Vesuvius, winemakers are rediscovering the grapes of antiquity but vinifying them in a modern style.

ITALY

CAMPANIA

TOP TERMS

Greco Bianco *(GREHK-oh bee-AHN-koh)*: This ancient *Greek white* variety is an *echo* of the Campanian wine industry that thrived eons *ago*. It makes zesty whites, with notes of grapefruit pith, chamomile, pear, and slate.
Campania *(kahm-PAHN-yah)*: If you're unfamiliar with wines from Campania, you are in good *company*. But this southern state's stock is rising rapidly as foodies and collectors discover its fine reinterpretations of ancient grape varieties.

DIGGING DEEPER

Irpinia *(eer-PEEN-ee-yah)*: Just east of Naples, Irpinia represents the *pinnacle* of Campania wine production. You might get a whiff of *gardenia* off the whites from the sloped vineyards in these foothills of the Appenines.
Tufo *(TOO-foh)*: Greco's best-known sub-zone in Irpinia is high on the mountainsides, where relatively cool temperatures and volcanic soils *toughen* the vines and build *toothsome* flavor in the Greco di Tufo white wines.

CULTURAL SNAPSHOT

Cicinelli, or *fragaglie* in Naples, are a Campanian delicacy. These briny morsels are fried in garlicky olive oil or incorporated into little savory pancakes called *fritelle* or *pizzelle*. Wash them down with Greco, Fiano, or Falanghina.

LANDMARK

The low-elevation vineyards around ancient Pompeii yielded super-ripe Greco, which Roman vintners dried before crushing and fermenting it. They aged this potent stuff, called Falernian, in pine-sap-sealed amphorae for more than a decade, then often diluted it with sea water, herbs, and other unguents before serving.

DON'T STOP THERE

Fiano *(fee-AH-noh)*: The grape behind the ancient Roman wine, Apianum. (That's Latin for *"bee," and so* it's fitting that the wine's texture is waxy.) Notes of tropical fruit, toasted nuts, lemon peel, and smoky spice complement a mouthfeel as slick as Billy Joel on the *piano*.

Falanghina *(FAH-lahn-GHEE-nah)*: Another component in ancient Roman Falernian, Falanghina creates a *phalanx* of flavor: sea brine, fennel, and pineapples *falling from the tree*.

Coda di Volpe *(KOH-dah dee VOHL-pay)*: It sounds like the *"code of the wolf,"* but actually, this grape is named "fox tail," because of its long, bushy-shaped clusters. It's often blended with Greco and Falanghina to make a citrusy, herbaceous wine with notes of apricot.

Lacryma Christi del Vesuvio *(lah-KREE-mah KREE-stee del veh-SOO-vee-yoh)*: On the lower slopes of *Mt. Vesuvius*, *Christ* apparently shed tears (*lacrimae* in Latin), and delicious grapes grew. The whites are blends of Coda di Volpe or Verdecca, with the addition of Falanghina or Greco.

A Pompeii mural devoted to wine

Rudimentary wood trellises support these southern Italian grapevines

EXTRA CREDIT

MORE CAMPANIA WHITE WINE SUB-ZONES

Capri *(KAH-pree)*: Romantic island off the Sorrento Peninsula in the Tyrrhenian Sea that specializes in Greco and Falanghina.

Costa d'Amalfi *(KOH-stah dah-MAHL-fee)*: The coastline east of Capri produces white wines from Falanghina plus the grape Biancolella.

Falerno del Massico *(fah-LAIR-noh del MAH-see-koh)*: Coastal region around the town of Mondragone where the whites are mostly Falanghina.

Fiano di Avellino *(fee-AH-noh dee ah-vell-EE-noh)*: Crisp, very fine Fiano-based whites grown in the foothills of the Apennines in Irpinia.

Galluccio *(gah-LOOCH-yoh)*: Around the town of Galluccio, northeast of Falerno del Massico, this region bases its whites on the Falanghina grape.

SANTORINI ASSYRTIKO

Greece dangles into the Mediterranean like a jellyfish floating with the tide, its tentacles trailing. Among the most southerly tentacles, aka the Aegean Islands, the most prominent wine production zone is sun-baked Santorini (SAN-toh-REE-nee). *Its scythe shape is a reminder that winemaking here dates back to the earliest days of civilization.*

GREECE

SANTORINI

KEY PLAYERS

Assyrtiko *(ah-SEER-tee-koh)*: An *assertive* white grape, Assyrtiko is the standard-bearer for the island of Santorini. It makes a relatively high-alcohol white that tends to be dry and deceptively simple. However, fresh acidity and zesty citrus-rind notes on the finish hint at Assyrtiko's depth. It also makes haunting dessert wines.

Athiri *(ah-THEE-ree)*: On the Aegean island of Rhodes, Athiri is made into Retsina, that pine-resin-flavored plonk that prevails in so many Greek restaurants. (There's *a theory* that Retsina was invented by the ancient Romans, who sealed their amphorae with pine resin.) Without the pine, on Santorini, Athiri makes a lemony, low-acid white wine that's a bit *dreary* on its own but complementary when blended with Assyrtiko.

DIGGING DEEPER

Crete *(KREE-tee; KREET in English)*: Just south of the Aegeans—and often lumped together with them—Crete is another island that's noted for its dry white wines

CULTURAL SNAPSHOT

If your mental image of Santorini is just sun, *sand and bikinis*, you might wonder how wine grapes can grow here. In fact, Santorini is only hot during the summer; cooler temperatures and rainfalls in the off seasons quench the thirsty volcanic soils.

made from indigenous grapes that probably date back to the beginning of *creation*. Crete also produces notable *sweet* wines.

Vinsanto *(vin SAHN-toh)*: An amber, apricot-nectar-like sweet and/or fortified dessert wine that's typically an Assyrtiko blend-based. It's similar to the Tuscan wine of the same name, but the Greek version came first; it is, after all, named after *Santorini*.

LANDMARK
Like the indigenous white grape varieties of the Greek islands, the picturesque Santorini village of Oia is historic, sturdy, white, and carved out of volcanic rock.

GEO QUIZ
Peloponesse *(PEH-loh-POH-neess-eh)*: On a map, the large peninsula hanging off southwestern mainland Greece looks like a hand, *pelting pieces* of rock into the Aegean Sea. It's noted for its red, particularly in the sub-zone of **Nemea** *(neh-MAY-uh)*. Also in the Peloponesse, **Patras** *(PAH-trahss)* is known for whites and dessert wines.

Macedonia *(MAAK-eh-DOH-nee-ah; MASS-eh-DOH-nee-ah)*: This northern Greek state (don't confuse it with the nation by the same name) is shaped like an upside-down bat with the head of a *mastedon.* Its sub-region of **Naousa** *(NOW-sah)* is known for red wines.

Yes, wine grapes do grow in paradise

Oia looks even more amazing after a glass of Assyrtiko

RUEDA VERDEJO

The Duero (DWAIR-oh) region shares four letters with its Rueda (roo-EH-dah) sub-zone. If you think of the "A" in Rueda as standing for "armpit," it's easy to find this wine region on a map. Because the Duero River, like a fresh, clean stick of deodorant, *heads inland from under Spain's west arm to Rueda.*

RUEDA

SPAIN

JOSÉ PARIENTE

KEY PLAYERS

Verdejo *(behr-DEH-hoh)*: Rueda's predominant white grape can be made into a lightweight, slurp-on-the-*veranda* wine with *verdant* notes of Granny Smith apple and lemon *verbena*. But given some time in barrel, it can be rich and creamy, with nut-and-mineral flavors.

Viura *(bee-OO-rah)*: Verdejo is prone to turn Sherry-like when exposed to oxygen. Viura, also called Macabeo *(MAHK-ah-BEH-oh)*, keeps its delicate notes of apples, white peaches, and flowers whether it's sealed in a tank or out in the open air. So, like *Viagra,* Viura keeps things perky when Verdejo gets a dose of it.

TOP TERMS

Castilla y León *(kah-STEE-yah ee leh-OHN)*: Like a bulky *Casaba melon* next to a compact honeydew, a white Verdejo labeled with the larger Castilla y Léon designation tends to be less expensive, with simpler flavors, than one from the Rueda sub-zone.

Rueda Superior: Not necessarily *superior*, because this

CULTURAL SNAPSHOT

Castile, or "land of castles," has always played an important role in Spanish history. The Castilian dialect of Castilla y León is the standard tongue of the nation of Spain. Likewise, Rueda Verdejo is, arguably, Spain's most prominent dry white wine.

Castillo de la Mota is nearly a thousand years old

word on a wine label simply guarantees that at least
85 percent of the grapes in the blend are Verdejo.
A basic "Rueda" can consist of just 50 percent Verdejo.

LANDMARK

The traditional wines of Rueda were fortified (with
brandy) as were the castles of Castilla y León. Castillo
de la Mota, just south of the town of Rueda, dates back
to the era when winemaking began in this region. It
was restored in the twentieth century, just a few decades
before Rueda winemakers gave up on fortification and
started making dry white wines from Verdejo.

DIGGING DEEPER

Sauvignon Blanc *(SOH-vee-nyoh BLAH)*: This French
grape *sews* tart grapefruit notes and resonating acidity
to Verdejo. The two grapes make a beautiful *violin*
concerto when they are *blended* together to make
a white wine in Rueda.

Verdelho *(vur-DELL-oh)*/**Malvasia** *(MAHL-bah-ZEE-*
ah): It's important that we *verify* that the Verdelho grape
is NOT the same thing as Verdejo. It goes by "Godello"
in eastern Galicia, where it's the top white. Ubiquitous
Malvasia, important in Italy, Portugal, Greece, and other
nations, gets around like *malaria* and happens to be
blended with Verdejo in Spain.

HUNTER VALLEY SEMILLON

Australia's most historic wine-growing region is located in the southeast corner of the country, near the iconic city of Sydney, where it's possible to book a whale-watching cruise. And if the map of Australia is shaped like an obese whale (see the fins up top?), New South Wales is right over the eyeballs.

AUSTRALIA

HUNTER VALLEY
SYDNEY
NEW SOUTH WALES

TOP TERMS

Hunter Valley: New South Wales' top wine-growing region is a two-hour drive north of Sydney. It's just about as difficult to grow grapes in the hot, wet "Hunter," as it's called, as it is to hunt your own dinner. But Semillon is up to the challenge.

Semillon *(seh-mee-YOH)*: Hunter Valley Semillon experiences a spiritual awakening ("I see millions!") and reinvents itself following a fatuous youth. Break its lifespan into halves, or *semis*, and you get a tart, citrusy waif (typically low in alcohol) in the early years and *Yoda* (waxy, perplexing, profound) with age.

OTHER OPTIONS

Chardonnay *(SHAHR-doh-NAY)*: It's **hard** to grow delicate Chard in the hot, humid Hunter Valley—this kind of heat makes for a big, **hard**-bodied wine. So look for bottles from the cooler, northern Upper Hunter.

Shiraz *(shi-RAZZ)*: Hunters may prowl in the woods, but wood barrels aren't the point of Hunter Valley Shiraz.

CULTURAL SNAPSHOT

Like sunbathers and whale watchers on Bondi Beach, New South Wales Semillon starts out pale and turns *semi*-brown over time. Aficionados say this wine is at its best with a decade or more of age behind it.

Young Semillon grapes on the vine

Unlike the robust, peppery, smoky Shiraz you might be used to, it's a more *sheer* style, with foresty notes of wild berries and soft earth.

LANDMARK
Bringing to mind wind-filled sails on a schooner ship, the Sydney Opera House is New South Wales' most recognizable resident. Hunter Valley Semillon, too, is like a white sail: Crisp and brisk when brand-new, it yellows over time, but that patina of age symbolizes strength and character.

DIGGING DEEPER
Canberra *(KAN-brah)*: Dark Shiraz, blended with a bit of white Viognier, can take on *cranberry* notes in Canberra, as can the cool-climate Pinot Noirs of this region approximately 180 miles (290 km) southwest of Sydney.

Mudgee *(MUD-jee)*: The Great Dividing Range catches moisture, keeping the Hunter Valley humid and Mudgee, on its west side, dry enough for growing Shiraz and Cabernet Sauvignon. Ironically, it's Hunter Valley that's more *muddy*.

YARRA VALLEY CHARDONNAY

Slicing a small wedge into Australia's southeastern coast, the Australian state of Victoria looks like the profile of the tiara of young Victoria, Queen of England. She surely would have enjoyed this region's liquid gold, Chardonnay.

AUSTRALIA

VICTORIA

YARRA VALLEY

TOP TERMS

Chardonnay *(SHAHR-doh-NAY)*: The sunny Chardonnays of Victoria's Yarra Valley tend toward juicy notes of *yellow* fruits—*yellow* plums, pears, nectarines, pineapple, starfruit—mellowed by the moderate use of oak barrels, which lend spice and roundness to the wines.

Yarra *(YAIR-ah)* **Valley**: The words "Yarra" and "yellow" sound mighty similar when uttered by a native Australian. You might have trouble telling the two apart. Which is how you'll remember that Yarra is famous for its *"yellah"* wine. Upper Yarra Valley Chardonnay country is up in the cool *air* at 1,200 feet (366 meters) in elevation.

OTHER OPTIONS

Pinot Noir *(PEE-noh NWAHR)*: What's yellow and black? Yarra (yellah) noir. Everyone's buzzing about the fresh, raspberry- and cherry-perfumed Pinot from the Upper Yarra. It's the bee's knees.

Sparkling Wine: Chardonnay and Pinot Noir are the two key components of Champagne. Accordingly,

CULTURAL SNAPSHOT

Queen Victoria wore a yellow cape in her coronation portrait and went by the title "Empress of India." And golden Chardonnay can be nearly as spicy as a yellow Indian curry when it comes from the Yarra Valley in Victoria.

Eureka Tower, Melbourne

Champagne-style bubbly has popped up in the Yarra Valley. Bees buzz; yellow-and-black Yarra goes "fizz."

LANDMARK

In bustling Melbourne, board the lift at Eureka Tower, the world's tallest residential building. Alight at level eighty-eight, and enjoy the views of the Yarra River; the Royal Botanic Gardens; and Queen Victoria Market (aka "Queen Vic"), where you can purchase Yarra Valley produce and taste wine.

DIGGING DEEPER

Heathcote *(HEETH-kut)*: The wind-buffeted foothills of the Great Dividing Range specialize in Shiraz that's as dark and hot-headed as *Heathcliff* roaming the moors in his *coat*.

Mornington Peninsula: The bracing winds of Mornington Peninsula are like a constant *morning* breeze thanks to the water (of Port Phillip Bay and Bass Straight) that surrounds it. As with the Yarra Valley, the cool conditions on this peninsula just south of Melbourne are ideal for growing Chardonnay and Pinot Noir.

Shiraz *(shi-RAZZ)*: Heady Heathcote breaks from its cool neighbors by specializing in *sizzling* Shiraz, dark and moody with notes of black pepper, spice, and smoke.

HAWKE'S BAY CHARDONNAY

New Zealand's North Island is shaped like a white shirt hanging on a clothesline, flapping in the wind in the warm sunshine. While the South Island specializes in tart Sauvignon Blanc, the North basks in glamorous golden Chardonnay.

HAWKE'S BAY

NEW ZEALAND

TOP TERMS

Chardonnay *(SHAHR-doh-NAY)*: The temperate climate of the North Island makes for ripe, tropical-fruit-flavored Chardonnay. The pleasant postscript is a pop of acidity—a hallmark of the vineyards around the cool inland valleys and **harbor** of *Hawke's Bay*.

Hawke's Bay: A forgiving climate, plus more than twenty-five different soil types, allow for many different grape varieties to thrive here. With its valleys, rivers, and nature preserves, this is a great place to be a **hawk**.

GEO QUIZ

Gisborne *(GHIZ-buhn)*: The northern neighbor of Hawke's Bay fans west from Poverty Bay. Chardonnay rules the **biz** here, especially around the inland city of Ormond, where prized single-vineyard Chards are sourced from an escarpment (what kind of **gizmo** is that?) called the Golden Slope.

Auckland: The area surrounding the metropolis is dense with small wineries. Although robust reds like

CULTURAL SNAPSHOT

The smooth gray paddle crab, named for its paddle-shaped back legs, is a mainstay on NZ restaurant menus. North Islanders know that soft buttery Chard makes a better match than sour Sauv Blanc with this scrumptious crustacean.

Syrah dominate, Chardonnay and Pinot Gris do well around Kumeu, northwest of the city. Just don't ask for Sauvignon Blanc at the local wineries here, because that would be *awkward*.

LANDMARK

Visitors to New Zealand scratch their heads about Tomato Peak. It's supposedly just a thirty-minute drive from the charming art deco town of Napier, but where is it on the map? Then you figure it out—like so many places in New Zealand, it was named by the resident Maori tribe, who tell an engrossing creation story about it. So while you might say "tomato," the locals are actually saying "Te Mata." At any rate, the place is a paradise for hikers and mountain bikers, and offers *hawk's-eye* views of the diverse landscape of the Hawke's Bay growing region.

Sun and slopes make grape-growing easy in Hawke's Bay

DIGGING DEEPER

Pinot Gris *(PEE-noh GREE)*: While it arrived in New Zealand only just recently, Pinot Gris is so *pleasingly agreeable* when grown in the maritime vineyards of this island nation that it's now the third-most-planted grape. In Hawke's Bay and Gisbourne, it makes a spicy, silky, food-friendly wine, with notes of pear and star anise.

Aromatics: The so-called "aromatic" grape varieties, which include Pinot Gris, make white wines that just *smell really, really good*. In Gisbourne, it's worth calling out a couple of others—rich, spicy Gewurztraminer, and powerful Viognier.

Tomato, Te Mata

MARLBOROUGH SAUVIGNON BLANC

New Zealand's South Island looks like a wide-bottomed chunk of celery that's been chopped with a blunt knife. The fibrous top is Marlborough (MAHRL-broh), the region that's world-renowned for producing a wine that tastes like salad.

MARLBOROUGH

NEW ZEALAND

TOP TERMS

Sauvignon Blanc *(SOH-vin-YOH blahnk)*: In comparison with the subtle Sauv Blancs of France's Loire Valley, New Zealand's contemporary Blancs hit you in the *solar plexus*, like you're in the middle of a fast-paced *soccer* game and have been knocked off your feet into fresh-mown grass.

Awatere *(AH-wah-TEER) Valley*: If ever a wine could *awaken you*, it's *green-tea*-like Sauv Blanc from Awatere Valley. While the northern Wairau Valley grows more grapes, the awards tend to go to wines sourced from the southernmost, coolest, and driest of Marlborough's three sub-regions.

GEO QUIZ

Nelson: Marlborough's soft-spoken western neighbor makes slightly more restrained, erudite wines, something like the designs of mid-century modernist *George Nelson*.

Waipara *(WYE-prah) Valley*: Even though it's in bone-chilling Canterbury, Waipara is a protected valley, so

CULTURAL SNAPSHOT

New Zealanders have green thumbs. Horticulture is a national pastime, and the New Zealand Gardens Trust makes it possible for the public to visit some of the gardens of private homes. In Marlborough, Winterhome is one not to miss.

Queen Charlotte Sound is not the worst place to sip Sauvignon Blanc

vineyard owners don't feel the need to **pray** to a higher spirit to ask **why** the grapes aren't ripening.

LANDMARK
Water, wind, and sunshine make Marlborough Sauvignon Blanc like no other in the world. To get a good taste of all three, strap on your hiking boots and tromp along a section of the Queen Charlotte Track, a long trail that follows the line of Queen Charlotte Sound. It's part of the Marlborough Sounds, a group of waterways tangled up in a quagmire of fjords that account for a fifth of New Zealand's coastline.

DIGGING DEEPER
Wairarapa *(WYE-rah-RAH-pah)*: Just to confuse you, this region on the southern tip of the North Island has almost the same name as the previously mentioned sub-zone of Canterbury. **Why, why, why** must we **wrap** our minds around these enigmas? To add insult to injury, its best-known sub-zone is Martinborough, which sounds a lot like Marlborough. Well, just think of them this way: The **Marlboro Man** rides his horse in the south, and **Martin Scorsese** makes films in the north. **Steel guitar** is a hallmark of southern music, while **rap** is a northern genre. Warm Wairarapa grows Sauvignon Blanc grapes with notes of tropical fruit and flowers.

ENGLISH SPARKLING

Despite a winemaking history that can be traced back to the Roman occupation, the UK was long thought too chilly for producing quality wines. Then along came climate change. Today, while other parts of the planet suffer, southern England is just balmy enough to produce elegant Champagne-style sparkling wines.

UK

SOUTHERN ENGLAND

TOP TERMS

Chardonnay *(SHAHR-doh-NAY)*: *Chase* the thought of luscious California Chardonnay from your mind as it would be *hard* to achieve that sort of ripeness here. The subtle aromas of English Chard are more along the lines of *hay*—ideal for sparkling wines.

Pinot Meunier *(PEE-noh MUH-nyay)*: You can bet *money* that the third most-important grape in Champagne also factors into England's sparkling wines.

Pinot Noir *(PEE-noh NWAHR)*: Champagne's most important grape is delicate, but manages to survive in chilly England, where *merino* sweaters are abundant. When it's not in a sparkling wine or a dry rosé, it makes a *leaner*, lower-alcohol red, not at all like the black-tinted *Noir* from California.

KEY PLAYERS

Méthode Traditionnélle *(MAY-tuhd trah-DEES-yon-EHL)*: The same *traditional*, time-consuming *method* of making sparkling wine that is used in Champagne.

CULTURAL SNAPSHOT

How British is bubbly? James Bond sips Bollinger and Dom Pérignon. There's a special Pol Roger cuvée named after Sir Winston Churchill. And eight Champagne houses are official purveyors to the royal family. The Brits love their bubbles.

The white cliffs of Dover

Kent and Sussex: On a map of southern England, the two most celebrated wine-growing regions cover the far right—the *suffix* side. The county of Kent is 235 miles (378 km) northwest of Reims, which is considered the northernmost place in France where it's possible to make good wine. But don't think they **Kent**—they **can**!

LANDMARK

On the south coast of England, Dover's cliffs face France. They're stark-white evidence that the soil here is suitable for sparkling wines, since the famous soils of Champagne are chalky. And they're an announcement to the rest of the world that the key wine color for the UK is white.

OTHER OPTIONS

Bacchus: Like the *Roman god at an orgy*, Bacchus is a three-way hookup between Silvaner, Riesling, and Müller-Thurgau. Citrusy like Sauvignon Blanc, it's the most familiar-tasting example of the unusual white grape varieties that make still (not sparkling) wines in England.

Pinot Blanc *(PEE-noh blahnk)*: While it can be blended into bubblies, some English vintners believe that the **white** version of Pinot might **bloom** into the future of English varietal still wines.

Wales: A small wine industry is just becoming visible in this principality west of England.

CHAMPAGNE

South of Belgium and halfway between Paris and Luxembourg, Champagne is known for its chalky soils and chilly climate. These are ideal conditions for growing crisp, acidic grapes, which make great sparkling wines. But if you visit, pack a parka.

CHAMPAGNE

FRANCE

TOP TERMS

Blanc de Blancs *(BLAH duh BLAH)*: *White* Champagne made from *white* grapes—usually Chardonnay, sometimes Pinot *Blanc*.

Blanc de Noirs *(BLAH duh NWAH)*: A *white* Champagne made from *black* grapes, most often Pinot *Noir*. The juice is pressed off the skins before the pigment can pinken it, unless rosé is on the agenda.

KEY PLAYERS

Chardonnay *(SHAHR-doh-NAY)*: The acidity can poke at your palate like *shards* of a broken Champagne flute.

Pinot Meunier *(PEE-noh MUH-nyay)*: Once in a blue *moon* you see Meunier bottled on its own. It's almost always a component of a blend, bringing high-flying Pinot Noir and Chardonnay down to earth.

Pinot Noir *(PEE-noh NWAHR)*: Like keys on a *grand piano*, Champagne achieves elegance by playing black against white. Pinot Noir might be a *black* grape, but it makes white sparkling wine.

CULTURAL SNAPSHOT

The Widow (Veuve) Clicquot is always bundled up in layers because Champagne is damp and chilly. Back then cellars were so cold that fermentation was delayed. The result was a crisp wine with bubbles trapped inside the bottle.

Cézanne serves Champagne with fruit and cheese instead of dessert

LANDMARK

The Champagne region's most celebrated cheese is Chaource. Buttery and gooey, it's the ideal foil for the lazer-sharp bubbles and knife-sharp acidity of Champagne. Learn all about it at the Musée du Fromage in the town of Chaource (down in the Aube), or visit a restaurant in Champagne and order the two together.

MORE TERMS TO KNOW

Brut *(BROOT)*: No, it's not the driest style of Champagne Extra Brut, aka Brut Zero, is, and it's so tart that some people find it **brutish**.

Grande Marque *(GROHND mahr-k)*: One of the large houses that purchase fruit from many vineyards and **market** millions of cases of wine annually. Container ships **groan** under the weight of all those heavy bottles.

Grower: Also known as an RM, or **Récoltant Manipulant**, the grower is a small artisanal house that **grows** its own grapes rather than buying them from many other vineyards. Like everyone's little blue-furred friend **Grover**, grower Champagnes are one-of-a-kind.

NV: Non Vintage Champagnes, referred to in shorthand on wine lists as "NV," are blended from multiple vintages to achieve a consistent style year after year. They **envy** the prestige of the rarer vintage Champagnes.

ALSACE CRÉMANT

All of France makes sparkling wine, but Alsace (al-ZASS), on the German and Swiss borders, is latitudinally suited to it, being Champagne's eastern neighbor. Its chilly valley floor grows Riesling, Pinots Blanc and Gris, Auxerrois, Chard, and Pinot Noir to make more Crémant (KRAY-mahn) than any other French region.

ALSACE

FRANCE

CRÉMANT D'ALSACE

TOP TERMS

Crémant: Bottle-fermented according to méthode traditionnelle, as Champagne is, Crémant is among the *crème de la crème* of sparkling wines. A less-stringent category is mousseux (*MOO-suh*), which may or may not be méthode traditionnelle.

GEO QUIZ

Crémant de Bourgogne *(duh BOOR-GON-yuh)*: Burgundy grows Champagne's two top grapes, Pinot Noir and Chardonnay. It should be a major Crémant producer but *be on guard* against cheapie bubbles from here.
Crémant de Loire *(duh LWAH)*: It's easy to be *lured* to the Loire's Chardonnay and Cabernet Franc-based sparkling wines. There are also mousseux sparkling wines from the sub-zones of Saumur and Vouvray.
Crémant du Jura *(doo ZHOO-rah)*: This undiscovered *jewel* of eastern France between Alsace and Burgundy makes bubbly from Chardonnay, Pinot Noir, and Jura grapes like Poulsard and Trousseau.

CULTURAL SNAPSHOT

Alsatian carnaval beignets, called *schenkeles*, or *schangalas*, are an exception to the rule that dry, acidic sparkling wines are better with salads than sweets. Try a *schenkele* with a yeasty Crémant d'Alsace and you'll feel like celebrating, too.

Alsace holidays, insufferable for grinches, scrooges, and curmudgeons

LANDMARK

Gingerbread-architectured, snow-sprinkled Alsace does the holiday season right. Hit the Christmas Market in Strasbourg to stock up on baubles, snow globes, and ornaments. And be sure to take frequent breaks for Crémant d'Alsace and pastries.

DIGGING DEEPER

Blanquette de Limoux *(BLAHN-kett duh lee-MOO)*: *Lemurs* have freaky-looking eyes and live on the island of Madagascar. Thanks to cool mountain vineyard sites that poke up from a *blanket* of southern French heat, Limoux is an island of freakishly inexpensive sparkling wines. Crémant de Limoux is Chardonnay and Chenin Blanc; Blanquette is the name for Crémant made mostly from the rustic Mauzac grape.

Crémant de Bordeaux *(duh BOHR-doh)*: Shouldn't it *border* on the impossible to make a light bubbly in the land of powerful Cab Sauv and Merlot? But winemakers can work with thirteen grape varieties here, so the results can be all over the *board*.

Saint-Péray *(SAN pair-AY)* **Brut**: In the Northern Rhône, this village gets cold enough to make sparkling wine from slightly underripe Marsanne and Roussanne grapes. Go for labels marked Méthode Traditionnelle to avoid something that tastes like *sandpaper*.

EXTRA CREDIT

MÉTHODE ANCESTRALE

Méthode traditionnelle, used to make Champagne and Crémant, is a double-fermentation process that calls for extra doses of sugar or juice, aging on lees (spent yeast), and a turning-and-freezing routine. **Méthode ancestrale** is simpler: The wine is bottled before the first fermentation is complete, trapping carbon dioxide that otherwise would have been released. The finished wine is semi-sweet, cloudy, and more pétillant (semi-sparkling) than mousseux (fully sparkling).

In southern France, Gaillac and Limoux both make méthode ancestrale sparkling wines. As does Die, a town at the far-eastern edge of the Rhône Valley that makes Crémant as well as a méthode ancestrale-style **Clairette de Die**. In addition, Bugey, a region between Savoie and Jura, makes a pretty pink méthode ancestrale semi-bubbly called **Cerdon**.

VENETO PROSECCO

The Veneto (VEH-neh-toh), *home of prominent Prosecco* (proh-SEK-koh), *looks like a pointy-chinned witch, in billowing skirts and a squashed hat, riding a broomstick with the Gulf of Venice at her back. (Maybe she's saying, "Double, double, boil, and bubble.") She's surrounded by fellow bubbly regions Trentino-Alto Adige, Lombardy, and Emilia-Romagna.*

VENETO

ITALY

TOP TERMS

Prosecco: Italy's best-known bubbly; drink as fresh as possible due to the winemaking style and the delicacy of the Glera *(GLAIR-uh)* grape. Champagne drinkers might call Prosecco *prosaic*, but some would say the winemaking *process* represents progress.

DOCG: Cheap Prosecco can taste like tin foil. Better Prosecco is labeled "DOC," for *Denominazione di Origine Controllata*. Even better is "DOCG" Prosecco, which gets *Garantita* added to its title and need not be *doctored* with peach purée or Aperol, *got it*?

DIGGING DEEPER

Lambrusco *(laam-BROO-skoh)*: You know what's delicious with *lamb*? This *rouge* wine made in Lombardy and Emilia-Romagna from a variety of indigenous grapes. The yin to Prosecco's yang, Lambrusco is a fruity, crisp, spicy, sparkling red.

Moscato d'Asti *(moh-SKAH-toh DAH-stee)*: This gently sparkling (frizzante) wine comes from Piedmont. It's low

in alcohol and smells like a fruit salad made of ultra-ripe peaches and melons. It could be a *mosquito attraction*.

LANDMARK

The Conegliano School of Oenology, founded in 1876, was the birthplace of the Italian or Charmat Method for turning flat wine into bubbly wine. Still white wine, sealed in pressurized tanks, ferments a second time, making crisp bubbles. By contrast, Méthode Champenoise requires a second fermentation inside each bottle. It's more labor-intensive and the resulting wine is more opulent, fruity, and yeasty.

DON'T STOP

Franciacorta *(FRAAN-chah-KOHR-tah)*: Perhaps this part of Lombardy is populated with *Francophiles* because its yeasty, bottle-fermented bubblies are similar to Champagne.

Trento Brut *(TRENT-oh BROOT)*: Deliciously inexpensive Champagne-style sparkling wine from a region north of the Veneto called Trentino-Alto Adige. Along with the Veneto and Friuli-Venezia Giulia, it makes up a *triangle* of excessively wordy northern wine regions that are often lumped together (see also p.48).

Brachetto d'Acqui *(brahk-ETT-oh DAHK-wee)*: It's difficult to *bracket* this low-alcohol, sweet, fizzy red wine from Piedmont without sounding *academic*— should you drink it with dessert or would it be better with breakfast?

Vineyards on the outskirts of Conegliano

EXTRA CREDIT

BUBBLES ON THE MARCHES

From north to south, almost every Italian region produces a **spumante** *(spoo-MAHN-tay)*—sparkling—wine. We've just met the best-known bubblies, but there are a few more worth knowing about. In Piedmont, for example, there's a bottle-fermented sparkler similar to Franciacorta. Made from Pinot Noir and Chardonnay, it's labeled **Alta Langa** *(AHL-tah LAAN-gah)*.

The state of **Marches**—**Marche** *(MAHR-kay)*, in Italian—along with its southern neighbor **Abruzzo** *(ah-BROOT-zoh)*, on central Italy's Adriatic (east) coast, are beginning to make a *mark* with their diverse array of wines from native grapes. The following are a few to know:

The lemony white **Verdicchio** *(vair-DEEK-ee-yoh)* grape, sometimes blended with other white grapes, makes crisp, dry bubblies.

The **Vernaccia Nera** *(vair-NAH-chah NAIR-ah)* grape makes a Lambrusco-like red sparkling wine, ranging from dry to sweet.

Brave winemakers turn **Passerina** *(PAH-ser-EE-nah)*, a rare and quirky indigenous white grape, into a bubbly that runs the gamut from thin and acidic to honeyed and rustic.

PENEDÈS CAVA

If Catalonia is the business section of a sparkling wine flute, Penedès (peh-neh-DEZ) is a bubble stuck to the side of the glass. Deliciously poised between the cities of Barcelona and Tarragona on the Mediterranean coast, this place would be fun even if it weren't awash with bottles of fizz.

PENEDÈS

SPAIN

TOP TERMS
Cava *(KAH-bah)*: Spanish sparkling wine is named after the cellars—*caves*—where it is made. It might taste a bit more rustic than Champagne, but it's priced so enticingly that you could supply a whole **cavalcade**.
Brut *(BROOT)*: High-acidity Brut wines are balanced by small amounts of sugar. The even-drier, leaner Brut Nature and Extra Brut styles can be **brutal** on the palate if paired with dessert, but make terrific apéritifs. Confusingly, *seco* and extra *seco* (dry and extra dry) Cavas are actually off-dry, with a bit of sweetness.

KEY PLAYERS
Macabeo *(MAHK-ah-BEH-oh)*: Vigorous, hardy, and found in just about every Cava bottle, Macabeo is a failsafe grape, as reliable as a box of **macaroni and cheese**. Under the name Viura, it's also the grape behind Rioja's sturdy, floral still white wines, which can handle some oak age.

CULTURAL SNAPSHOT
A typical Barcelona New Year's Eve entails a light-and-music spectacle, the custom of eating a good-luck grape every *campanada* (three seconds) for the twelve seconds prior to midnight, red underwear, and free-flowing Cava.

A hotel near Barcelona designed as a stack of sparkling wine bottles

Xarel-lo *(CHAH-reh-LOH)***/Parellada** *(PAH-reh-YAH-dah)*: The grape *charged* with bringing *sharpness* and *cha cha* to Cava, Xarel-lo brims with notes of apples, fennel, and honeycomb. The third grape of Cava, Parellada does not *parallel* its peers.

LANDMARK

Meta moment: sipping Cava while standing inside a bottle of sparkling wine. Or, at least you'll feel this way when you're in the tasting room at Cava & Hotel Mastinell, about an hour east of Barcelona. Designed to look like a stack of wine bottles, this contemporary masterpiece suggests the works of famed Barcelonan architect Antoni Gaudí. Fittingly, it looks out over a vineyard.

DIGGING DEEPER

Rosado *(roh-SAH-doh)*: **Garnacha** *(gahr-NAH-chah)* and **Monastrell** *(MOH-nah-STRELL)* are used for their robust ripe-berry notes and vibrant color, while the native **Trepat** *(treh-PAHT)* keeps the alcohol pleasantly low, in *rosé* (pink) rosados.
Reserva *(reh-SAIR-bah)*: Basic Cava ages in the winery cellar for at least nine months prior to release. Reserva is *reserved* at least fifteen months; and Gran Reserva more than thirty months.

TAVEL ROSÉ

In the Southern Rhône Valley, just northwest of Avignon and Provence, Tavel is world-famous for making wine that's pink and no other color. And to Tavel's south and west, there are many more realms of rosé production. Together, they surround a sunny C-shaped bay on the Mediterranean. This is pink wine country.

FRANCE

NORTHERN RHÔNE
SOUTHERN RHÔNE
TAVEL

TOP TERMS

Tavel/Lirac *(TAH-vell/LEE-rak)*: Bright as a **Tab** cola can and potent as a red Rhône wine, Tavel fits on the **table** with anything from salad to steak. Lirac, Tavel's northern neighbor, makes a Tavel-like rosé that tends to be less expensive. Which one would presidential embezzler *Jacques Chirac* order?

Costières de Nîmes *(KOHS-tyair duh NEEM)*: Alongside the city of Nîmes, the southwesternmost point of the Rhône Valley bumps into Provence and the Languedoc. The fruity, dry rosés don't **cost nearly** as much as those of Tavel, but then again, they aren't nearly as intense.

KEY PLAYERS

Grenache *(gruh-NASH)*/**Grenache Blanc** *(BLAH)*: Grenache gives Tavel its signature vermilion glow and cherry-cranberry flavor. And although it's not legal to blend finished white and red wines to make rosé in France, it is legal to **mash** red and white Grenache grapes together.

CULTURAL SNAPSHOT

Camargue horses are small in stature, tough by nature, and, like rosé wine, rare but beloved. They have black skins but white coats, making them appear gray, just as the pink drink of this part of France is made from a black-skinned grape.

The Salin d'Aigues Mortes turns an unexpected pink every summer

Syrah/Mourvèdre/Cinsault/Carignan *(SEE-rhah; sih-RAH/MOOR-ved-ruh/SAN-soh/CAH-ree-NYOH):* Four more grapes commonly found in southern French rosés. Just remember: SMCC. *Save my sins for confession* tomorrow because I'm too busy drinking rosé today to bother feeling guilt.

LANDMARK

For more than two thousand years, precious *fleur de sel* has been collected at the Salin d'Aigues Mortes by hand. Algae turns the saline water pink as it evaporates in the heat; this environment attracts an abundance of wildlife, including, appropriately, pink flamingoes.

GEO QUIZ

Languedoc *(LONG-dok):* **Long docks** poke out into the Mediterranean throughout this coastal region in south-central France. It's less popular with tourists than Provence, and this might explain, in part, why the simple pink wines tend to sell for a *lot less ducats.*

Sud-Ouest/Gascogne *(SOOD west/GAS-koh-nyha):* This mishmash of generally hot and dry wine regions makes up the **southwest** of France, and its unusually named indigenous grapes make sturdy, rustic pink wines. Gascony, aka Gascogne, where brawny Tannat dominates the rosé, is so affordable you'll *gasp* at the prices.

PROVENCE BANDOL MOURVÈDRE

The south of France undulates in a W-shape, like a pair of waves on the Mediterranean Sea. Provence's wine-growing region occupies the trough and upward slopes of the second wave, jutting into the Mediterranean between the cities of Avignon and Nice.

FRANCE

PROVENCE

TOP TERMS

Bandol *(BAHN-dohl)*: France's most distinguished rosé region, known for structured wines built from a base of Mourvèdre. The best Bandols can be quite pricey in comparison to other pink wines, so be prepared to *bankroll* your taste for Bandol.

Côtes de Provence *(KOHT duh PROV-ahnss)*: The largest wine-producing region in Provence, it's a *coat* over a big swath of land, mostly to the east. Its counterpart on the west side is **Coteaux d'Aix en Provence** *(KOHT-oh DEX uhn PROV-ahnss)*.

KEY PLAYERS

Mourvèdre *(MOOR-ved-ruh)*: This ornery, tannic grape makes a mean, blackish-red wine in Bandol. It's a tougher job for winemakers to coax pretty pink juice from it, but the payoff comes in layers of herbaceous, savory intrigue. This is a rosé that requires *more involved* winemaking and a wine that you'll find yourself becoming more and *more involved* with.

CULTURAL SNAPSHOT

Why didn't the girls in the "Bain du Soleil" ads ever have unsightly tan lines? Because Saint-Tropez is famous for its nude beaches. Sadly, it's peopled by naturist northerners, making this part of Provence as well-known for its pink skin as for its pink wines.

Rose-colored glasses are not necessary at the seaside town of Bandol

Grenache *(gruh-NASH)*: Yang to Mourvèdre's yin in Bandol is thin-skinned, fruity Grenache. If you're getting *more involved* with someone and he *bankrolls* a trip to New York, maybe add some fun variety to your stay by strolling around *Greenwich Village*.

LANDMARK

The sandy beaches at Bandol, clustered in a couple of warm, protected harbors, can look as pink as the town's stucco storefronts at sunrise and sunset. Needless to say, just about every wine glass in every beachfront café here is filled with Bandol rosé during the summer months.

MORE KEY PLAYERS

Syrah *(SEE-rhah; sih-RAH)*: You might *see red* when you read Syrah, but surprisingly, this spicy, tannic grape makes terrific pink wine, often with notes of grapefruit and white pepper.

Cinsault *(SAN-soh)*: Thin-skinned and not very tannic, Cinsault is the grape *sans (without) a soul*, adding fragrance but not gravity to Provençal rosé blends.

Grenache Gris *(gruh-NASH GREE)*: The most-common form of Grenache is also called Grenache Noir, because its skins are bluish black. Its sibling, Gris, has *gray* (more like pink, really) skins—perfect for making pink wine.

ROSÉ **95**

CORSICA PATRIMONIO NIELLUCCIO

Corsica, the island south of France and west of Italy, is shaped like a left foot, with a peninsula poking north like a big toe and wine regions surrounding its periphery like a slipper. Arguably, its most exquisite offerings are as pink as a bare foot on a beach.

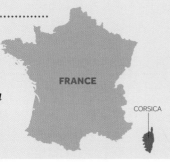

FRANCE

CORSICA

TOP TERMS

Ajaccio *(AH-zhahk-SHOH)*: The island's most prominent sub-zone, *adjacent* to the west coast Corsican capital of the same name.

Patrimonio *(PAT-ree-MOH-nyoh)*: The first official appellation on Corsica with a history of wine-growing going back hundreds of years (that's *patrimony*). This northern district gets surprisingly cool and foggy, making it a renowned region for Vermentino (white) grapes as well as reds and rosés with crisp acidity.

KEY PLAYERS

Nielluccio *(NEE-ay-LOOCH-oh)*: Closely related to Italian Sangiovese, Nielluccio is the most prevalent grape in Patrimonio and on the island as a whole. It has a leathery, savory aroma—when blended with pale, delicate Sciaccarellu, it's like a *Neanderthal* who has bathed with scented soap and used a *loofah*.

Sciaccarellu *(see-AH-kah-RELL-oo)*: The key red grape of Ajaccio and the second grape of the island of

CULTURAL SNAPSHOT

Corsica has ping-ponged between empires throughout history, mostly against the will of its people. So while it's part of France, this island flies its own flag (right), symbolizing the renegade Corsican spirit.

Eight-thousand-year-old menhir statues at Filitosa

Corsica, it's pale-skinned and must be blended to make a convincing red. (Sort of like when you *see a karaoke-ing fool* who would sound better if they weren't solo.) But it makes an herbaceous wine, fragrant with stone fruit and citrus rind, when the juice is pressed off the skins to make rosé.

LANDMARK

Filitosa is an eight-thousand-year-old archaeological site where visitors can view menhirs carved into primitive statues by prehistoric Corsicans. Like the unique wine grapes of Corsica, it's ancient and mysterious. It's a dry, rocky spot positioned up in the hills above the sea, just as nearby vineyards are, for the cooler temperatures. And the countryside here is covered with the wild herbs of the *maquis* (shrubland) and olive trees—two common aromatic descriptors for Corsica's wines.

DIGGING DEEPER

Île de Beauté *(EEL duh BOH-tay)*: Geographic designation for wines sourced from grapes grown anywhere on the whole *beautiful island.*
Ajaccio *(AH-zhahk-SHOH)*: The island's most prominent sub-zone, *adjacent* to the west coast Corsican capital of the same name. By contrast, the top Corsican rosés are *pressed directly* from the grapes.

LOMBARDY CHIARETTO

There are increasingly interesting pockets of pink production scattered in every region of Italy. North-central Lombardy and neighboring Veneto guard a secret around the banks of Lago di Garda: Chiaretto. A wine-growing style that straddles both regions, this peppy pink shows up more often in stores and wine lists than in books.

TOP TERMS

Chiaretto *(KEE-ah-RAY-toh)*: Made from a blend of red grapes, this rose-petal-pink wine is aromatic with floral and wild-berry perfume. Often frizzante (lightly sparkling), it won't cause you to **keel over** since it tends toward lower alcohol.

Garda/Bardolino *(GAHR-dah/BAHR-doh-LEE-noh)*: In Lombardy, Chiaretto comes from the growing region on the southwest bank of the Lago di **Garda**. In the Veneto, Chiaretto comes from Bardolino, which **borders** the southeast side of the lake.

DON'T STOP

Rosato di Toscana *(rohs-AH-toh dee toh-SKAH-nah)*: **Tuscany** dominates the Italian wine industry, so it should come as no surprise that a paler version of savory Sangiovese from Tuscany rules the rosato sector as well.

Cerasuolo d'Abruzzo *(CHAY-rah-SWOH-loh dee ah-BROOT-zoh)*: It means "**cherry colored**" in the Abruzzo dialect, but sounds—disturbingly—more like **cheery,**

CULTURAL SNAPSHOT

Any Italian wine region that grows red grapes can make pink wine. But in only a few places is rosé considered a local specialty. That's why those with their own special rosato appellations, like Chiaretto, are worth watching.

swollen, and bruised. At any rate, this flamingo-pink, juicy wine is made from the Montepulciano grape.

LANDMARK

Sirmione is built on a long narrow spit that juts into the Lago di Garda. Cascades of bougainvillea turn the whole town a pronounced pink during the warm season.

DIGGING DEEPER

Salento Negroamaro *(sah-LENT-oh NAY-groh-ah-MAH-roh)* **Rosato**: Down in the heel of the boot of Italy, in the Salento zone of Puglia, the black-skinned Negroamaro grape makes a rosato with lip-smacking *salinity*. It's so hot-pink it could be *nail polish*.
Sicilia Nerello Mascalese *(see-CHEEL-ya neh-RELL-oh mahss-kah-LAY-zay)* **Rosato**: On the isle of *Sicily*, the dark Nerello Mascalese grape is grown in the *elemental* volcanic soils *near* the peak of Mt. Etna. Let's hope the vineyards won't be *massacred* by *magma*, because the rosato is quite good.

Lombardy's capital is fashionable Milan

Yes, there is a building underneath that bougainvillea in Sirmione

NAVARRA ROSADO

Navarra (nah-BAH-rah) *is the name of a state and a wine region in north-central Spain that's shaped like an abstract glass of wine. Actually, it's more like a big, fat chalice—which would be an appropriate vessel for Navarra rosado, a wine that is eminently gulp-able. It's just one of Spain's many delicious pinks.*

NAVARRA

SPAIN

GEO QUIZ
Navarra: The mostly Garnacha-based pink blends of Navarra are often topped off with a bit of Merlot, Tempranillo, or Cabernet Sauvignon. Your basic inexpensive Navarra rosado is a watermelon-hued soda-like treat, dripping with flavors of *navel* orange and ripe cherry.

Rioja *(ree-OH-hah)*: The Tempranillo grapes of Navarra's western neighbor make rosados that are *real* treats, with notes of nectarine and citrus rind. And they're so affordable that you'll laugh, "*Oh, hah!*" when you get the bill.

KEY PLAYERS
Garnacha *(gahr-NAH-chah)*: Garnacha *garners* the gorgeous color and irresistible strawberry-cherry-rose-petal notes of *Jennifer Garner* ... I mean Navarra rosado.

Tempranillo *(TEM-prah-NEE-yoh)*: Many wine lovers consider Rioja's Tempranillo-based rosados to be the *template* by which all other rosés should be measured.

CULTURAL SNAPSHOT
The official DO—or Designation of Origin—"Navarra" is also printed on *espárrago blanco* (white asparagus) labels. Buy it fresh in Navarra's farmers markets in the spring, just around the time that new rosado vintages hit store shelves.

Not only are they immensely satisfying, but they are not overpriced. Serve them at a cool but not cold temperature to savor their flavors.

LANDMARK

The Vías Verdes (greenways) of Spain are old railway lines that have been resurrected as public hiking and biking paths. In Navarra, the Vía Verde del Tarazonica follows the path of the Ebro River to the foot of Monte Moncayo and the surrounding nature reserve. In the afternoon sun, when the dirt road begins to look pink, it's time to stop, take that bottle of rosado out of your backpack and plunge it in the river to chill.

Yes, blue grapes can make pink wine

DIGGING DEEPER

Cigales *(thee-GAHL-ess)*: Hot as the tip of a *cigar*, the Cigales sun gets Tempranillo and Garnacha super-duper ripe. This wine-growing zone in northern Spain, just west of Ribera del Duero, has a long tradition of making boldly colored, super-fruity, inexpensive pink picnic wines.

Txakolí *(CHAH-koh-LEE)*/**Cava** *(KAH-bah)*: Although we cover these wines in the Delicate White and Sparkling sections, it's worth repeating that they both come in shades of pink as well as white. Txakolí is typically semi-sparkling and quite dry, with notes of red currants and cranberry. Fully sparkling rosado Cava is like rosé Champagne's country cousin, with notes of honeycomb, lemon peel, and raspberry.

Growing conditions in the Canary Islands are, to put it mildly, challenging

WILLAMETTE VALLEY PINOT NOIR

Like its southern neighbor California, Oregon (OH-reh-gun) *covers a lot of ground—it's larger than the entire United Kingdom—but its wine country mostly follows a north to south trajectory parallel to the coastline.*

UNITED STATES

WILLAMETTE VALLEY

OREGON

TOP TERMS

Pinot Noir *(PEE-noh NWAHR)*: Easygoing Oregon Pinot is, like a comfy flannel shirt, the midpoint between the Burgundian silk *peignoir* style and a black, dense California wetsuit, featuring firm acidity, fresh-fruit notes of raspberry and blackberry, and earthy, woodsy aromas.
Willamette *(wil-AM-it)* **Valley**: This long, lean region follows the path of the Willamette River from Portland to Eugene, encompassing six sub-zones. Protected from the Pacific Ocean by the Coast Range, the Willamette Valley enjoys mild weather, *dammit*!

GEO QUIZ

Dundee Hills/Chehalem *(shuh-HAIL-em)* **Mountains/Ribbon Ridge**: In the northeast corner of the valley, the red-soiled Dundee Hills make velvety Pinots with red-fruit flavors and *dusty* tannins. And we *should all hail the* diverse soil types and elevations of the Chehalem Mountains and *tie a bow* on the small gift that is the revered Ribbon Ridge.

CULTURAL SNAPSHOT

The Pacific Northwest's wild, orange-fleshed salmon are so strong that they swim many thousands of miles in their short lifespans—and their flavor is so strong that it overwhelms white wines. Earthy Oregon Pinot Noir to the rescue.

"Forest floor" is a common descriptor for Pinot Noir

Yamhill-Carlton/McMinnville *(mik-MIN-vil)/***Eola-Amity** *(ee-OH-lah AM-it-ee)* **Hills:** The warm Yamhill-Carlton and McMinnville appellations turn out dark Pinots, fragrant with notes of roasted *yam*, clove, and *minced fennel*. And chilly nighttime winds off the Pacific are so strong in the Eola-Amity Hills that they could blow *Eeyore's* tail right off, *amassing acidity* in the grapes.

LANDMARK
When Oregonians smell "forest floor" in their Pinot, they aren't putting you on. Western Oregon is timber country—even in urban areas. Forest Park in the Tualatin Mountains cuts right through the city of Portland.

DON'T STOP THERE
Columbia Gorge: This *gorgeous* river canyon is lined with *columns* of basalt cliffs. The winds that barrel through the western end of this massive ravine suit cool-climate grapes like Pinot Noir, while easterly, semi-arid sites favor Rhône and Italian grape varieties.
Umpqua *(UHMP-kwah)* **Valley:** Just south of the southern Willamette Valley, the Umpqua encompasses *umpteen*-gazillion different microclimates. High-elevation, colder sites to the north cradle delicate varieties like Pinot Noir and Riesling, while southerly vineyards support hearty Tempranillo and Syrah.

SONOMA COAST PINOT NOIR

San Franciscans get some of the best local produce in the nation. The local wine isn't too bad, either. Sonoma County, and sub-zones Sonoma Coast and Russian River Valley, are hot spots for cool-climate Pinot Noir.

UNITED STATES

SONOMA COAST

CALIFORNIA

TOP TERMS

Pinot Noir *(PEE-noh NWAHR)*: It's maybe disingenuous to call California Pinot Noir a "Light Red," since unmitigated sunshine and lusty consumer appetites have sent the state Pinot style more toward black—*noir*—than the reddish-pink *peony* shade you'd see in Burgundy.

Sonoma Coast/Russian River Valley: These connected sub-regions get the *rushing* winds and *coastal* fogs that delicate Pinot Noir needs to maintain its *quivering* acidity and perky red fruit notes.

GEO QUIZ

Sta Rita Hills/Santa Lucia *(loo-SEE-yah)* **Highlands**: Two top Pinot zones, both in California's massive Central Coast region, with confusingly similar names. The Sta Rita Hills are down south, closer to *Santa* Barbara, where you might drink a *Margarita* at the beach. The Santa Lucia Highlands, *loosely* speaking, are in the *highlands* to the north, in the Monterey sub-region.

Central Coast/Santa Maria Valley: The Central Coast

CULTURAL SNAPSHOT

Locations for California's Pinot Noir film, *Sideways*, were in the Central Coast's Sta Rita Hills, Santa Maria Valley, and Santa Ynez Valley. To see the Sonoma Coast and Russian River Valleys' brooding scenery, catch Hitchcock's *The Birds*.

is so huge and, well, **central** to California's Pinot Noir movement that it's worth praising one more sub-zone named after a lady saint: the Santa Maria Valley, on the east side of the town of Santa Maria, just north of the Sta Rita Hills. Maybe if you think of them in alphabetical order, north to south you'll remember Lucia, Maria, and Rita. Now sing that, to the tune of "Mambo No. 5."

LANDMARK

How can California grow Pinot Noir, a notoriously fickle grape that can't handle heat? It's easy to forget that this state is nearly one-and-a-half times the size of Italy, so there's plenty of variation in climate and topography, accommodating a wide range of viticulture. To get a feel for the brisk ocean mists and morning fogs of the Sonoma Coast, take a hike at blustery Sonoma Coast State Park.

Small Pinot Noir grapes are big on flavor

DIGGING DEEPER

Anderson Valley/Mendocino *(MEN-doh-SEE-noh)*: Just as **Anderson Cooper vilifies mendacity**, the rural, forested, northerly Mendocino wine region is all about authenticity (there are a lot of earnest organic farmers here). The cool, damp Anderson Valley sub-zone grows delicate Pinot Noir grapes.

Carneros *(kahr-NAIR-ohss)*: This growing zone crosses the south ends of both the Napa and Sonoma Valleys and attracts fogs and brisk breezes off San Pablo Bay. If you're a **carnivore** who likes your Pinot Noir on the meatier end of the spectrum, check out Carneros.

Bundle up in warm layers before visiting Sonoma Coast State Park

CALIFORNIA BUBBLES

Sparkling wine is big business in California. And given that the top grapes of France's Champagne region are Pinot Noir and Chardonnay, it follows that California's best bubbles come from some of its top Pinot zones. The three to know: **Anderson Valley**, the pocket of cool in northerly Mendocino; Sonoma County's **Russian River Valley**; and **Carneros**, the growing zone that crosses the south ends of both Napa and Sonoma Valleys and attracts fogs and brisk breezes off San Pablo Bay. So when you think California sparkling, think **ARRVC**: "**A Rolls-Royce vacation** requires **Champagne**."

Insider tip: Some of California's most famous bubbly-producing wineries are owned by French Champagne houses.

BURGUNDY PINOT NOIR

If the nation of France were a person, facing you, with limbs outstretched, Burgundy would be its beating heart. The top Pinot Noir vineyards are located in the northern section, south of the city of Dijon and surrounding the town of Beaune—the region's vinous capital.

BURGUNDY

FRANCE

TOP TERMS

Côte d'Or *(KOHT dohr)*: Before you enter a house, you've got to hang your *coat by the door*… and before you learn about any other part of Burgundy, you've got to know the northerly Côte d'Or, which is composed of the Côte de Nuits to the north and the Côte de Beaune in the south.

Pinot Noir *(PEE-noh-NWAHR)*: Like a *film noir* it's mysterious, seductive, stylish, classic. And once you get a taste, you just can't stop thinking about it.

DIGGING DEEPER

Côte de Beaune *(KOHT duh BOHN)*: Burgundy's summers tend to be cool and rainy, making for wines with brisk acidity. So if you're planning to visit, pack a *coat* and prepare for *bone*-chilling cold.

Côte de Nuits *(KOHT duh NWEE)*: Like Sigmund Freud with his *goatee*, the head section of Burgundy makes the most expressive and cerebral wines, which is why there are so many Grand Cru vineyards here.

CULTURAL SNAPSHOT

Beef Bourguignon is braised in red wine, with mushrooms and lots of herbs. Earthy Bourgogne Rouge *(BOOR-GON-yuh ROOZH)* matches this dish well: It isn't overly fruity or spicy, but tends to be subtle, with earthy, herbaceous notes.

LANDMARK

Burgundy was made great by monks, like those at Fontenay Abbey, who for hundreds of years carefully studied cultivars, soil types, and winemaking techniques.

GEO QUIZ

Aloxe-Corton *(ah-LOHX-uh KOHR-tuhn)*: This village makes tart and fruity Pinots, like the red apples in that *luxe* gift *carton* you get at Christmas. (Côte de Beaune)

Chambolle-Musigny *(SHAHM-bol MOO-zin-yee)*: This commune's wines make you feel like *shambling* through a field of flowers, *musing about music*. (Côte de Nuits)

Gevrey-Chambertin *(juh-VRAY SHAHM-bare-TUH)*: As tough as the *shove* Sugar *Ray* Leonard would give to a *bear*. (Côte de Nuits)

Morey-St-Denis *(moh-RAY sahn de-NEE)*: Do you get *more sandy* on a more-famous beach? Then why would these less-famous wines be less flavorful? (Côte de Nuits)

Pommard *(POH-mahr)*: Often tough and tannic, it can *pummel* your palate hard. (Côte de Beaune)

Volnay *(VOHL-nay)*: *Full* of *floral* notes, silky as a *sleigh* gliding over soft snow. (Côte de Beaune)

Vosne-Romanée *(VOHN RHO-mahn-ee)*: Tasting this wine is akin to *phoning* the *Roman* god Jupiter, getting hit by lightning and going up in smoke. In a good way. (Côte de Nuits)

Fontenay Abbey, founded in 1118

BEAUJOLAIS GAMAY

In central-eastern France, the borders of Beaujolais (BOH-zhoh-LAY) are marked by Mâcon on the north and Lyon at the south. Like the red-headed stepchild of its northern and southern neighbors, Burgundy and the Rhône, Beaujolais wines can be fruity one minute and fierce the next.

FRANCE

BEAUJOLAIS

TOP TERMS

Gamay *(GAA-may)*: The red grape of Beaujolais. Nouveau-style Gamay is just plain happy, or ***gay***. It would be just fine out of a plastic cup, on ***game day***. Higher-quality Gamay, in a bottle marked "Cru" or "Villages," tastes a bit ***gamey***.

Nouveau *(NOO-voh)*: ***Never*** lay this ***new*** wine down to age. Thanks to a quick fermentation in an airtight vessel, juicy Nouveau ***glows*** a bright ruby-red and tastes like fruit punch. It's released just a couple of months after harvest and tastes best slightly chilled.

DIGGING DEEPER

Cru *(KROO)*: The term "Cru" denotes that the grapes were sourced from the finest vineyards in the region. There is a ***crew*** of ten Crus in Beaujolais; in the sport of rowing, also known as ***crew***, it's common to pull a "power ***ten***" of strong strokes to pass another boat.

Villages *(vee-LAHZH)*: Quality vineyard zones centered around Beaujolais' northern ***villages*** and towns, Villages

Le Beaujolais Nouveau est arrivé!

A windmill like no other, the Moulin-à-Vent of Beaujolais

wines can handle some cellar *age*. The wise *villagers* possess more depth of character than Nouveau, but they're a bit *cruder* than the Crus.

LANDMARK
One of Beaujolais' most famous Crus shares its name with a tourist stop: Moulin-à-Vent, the massive stone windmill (in French a *moulin-à-vent*) that overlooks many vineyards. Contrary to popular opinion about Beaujolais wines, Moulin-à-Vent Gamay is as stalwart as a stone tower, as powerful as a mill, and as bracing as a strong wind.

FOR CONTRARIANS
Beaujolais Blanc *(BOH-zhoh-LAY BLAH)*: White (*blanc*) Beaujolais is made mostly from the Chardonnay grape and can range from nice, easy-drinking white to *plonk*.

Sparkling Beaujolais: A few Beaujolais producers are playing around with double-fermenting juicy red Gamay to create something akin to fruit punch with bubbles. If you see it, try it!

LOIRE CABERNET FRANC

If France were a red STOP sign, the Loire Valley would skim the tops of the letters S and T. And while the Loire is best-known for its white statement wines, they stand out against an equally bold backdrop of fine reds, namely Cabernet Franc and Pinot Noir.

LOIRE

FRANCE

TOP TERMS

Cabernet Franc *(KAB-air-nay FRAHN)*: Best-known as a lesser blending grape in Bordeaux, Cabernet Franc is like the **cabal of General Franco** in the Central Loire, taking power here and reigning supreme.

Touraine *(TOO-rhen)*: The Central Loire macro-region of Touraine encompasses the smaller Cabernet Franc appellations of Chinon, Saumur, and Bourgueil as well as other red zones. It's like a spacious **Volkswagen Touareg**: You can pile the entire cabal of General Franco in there, and still have room for more.

GEO QUIZ

Chinon *(shee-NOHN)*, **Saumur** (SOH-myur*)*, **Bourgueil** (BOOR-gay*)*: Pour yourself a glass, put your hair up in a **chignon**, apply some red lipstick, and primp until you look **sooo** good in the **mirror**. Then go to the club to **boogie**. Because the Cabernet Francs from these Loire appellations are so invigorating that they'll make you feel like dancing the night away.

CULTURAL SNAPSHOT

Touraine is known as the "garden of France," as illustrated by the bounteous vegetable plots at the Château de Villandry. And the restrained red wines from this region complement a vegetarian menu beautifully.

Elegant cave living at Rochmenier Village Troglodytique

OTHER OPTIONS

Pinot Noir *(PEE-noh-NWAHR)*: The ethereal Pinots from the Loire's eastern section are as light as *pins* and piercing as *needles*.

Sancerre *(SAHN-sair)*: Pinot Noir from Sancerre tastes something like a tart glass of cranberry juice. Chill it in the fridge and serve it with a turkey *sandwich*.

LANDMARK

The Loire is famous for its *tuffeau*, a soft marine sedimentary stone thought to impart minerality to the wines of the region. It's also famous for what people have done with it—they've moved in. Rochmenier Village Troglodytique, a twenty-five-minute drive from Saumur, is a community carved out of caves, as unexpected and delightful as a red wine from the Loire.

DIGGING DEEPER

Cheverny *(SHUH-vair-nee)*: *Touring in a Chevrolet* is nice, but touring in a Cadillac is even nicer. In the Touraine village of Cheverny, workaday Gamay is blended with glamorous Pinot Noir to make reds that hit just the right gear.

Gamay *(GAA-may)*: In Touraine, in the mid-eastern Loire, Gamay makes a *gamma ray* of a red: a bright flash of color and electric acidity.

JURA POULSARD

If France were a woman's torso, the departement of Jura (ZHOO-rah) would occupy that spot on the eastern border where the narrow waist widens to meet the ribs. Like thin skin and protruding bones, cold temperatures and rocky outcroppings here make the wines lean and rangy.

FRANCE

JURA

TOP TERMS

Arbois *(AR-bwah)*: **Our boy** Arbois is a town surrounded by trellises, or, if you like, grape **arbors**, and the Jura's top appellation.

Poulsard *(POOL-sahr)*: Thin-skinned Poulsard is like the delicate younger sibling of Pinot Noir. Also spelled Ploussard, it's the opposite of those red wines that look like **pulsing blood**: rather, it's nearly as translucent as a **swimming pool**.

OTHER OPTIONS

Vin Jaune *(VAH zhohn)*: When the **members of the jury** *(the Jura?)* peruse a wine list together, the nonconformists vote for Vin Jaune. Like the title character in the courtroom comedy *My Cousin Vinny*, Vin Jaune is the crazy, uninhibited wine that breaks all the rules and gets away with it—it's yellow (*jaune* in French) and it's purposefully made to taste like Sherry, which would be a winemaking error in any other region. It's possibly the weirdest thing you will ever taste.

2009

Arbois

Appellation Arbois Contrôlée

Poulsard

CULTURAL SNAPSHOT

Ah, the fresh mountain air! The naturally saline thermal waters of Salins-les-Bains! The salubrious hikes in the Parc Naturel Régional du Haut-Jura! This is a healthful part of the world, and the wines are equally invigorating.

The vineyards of chilly Jura get their fair share of snow

Macvin du Jura *(MACK-vah doo ZHOO-rah)*:
A sweet, late-harvest wine. It may be a pretty shade of red, yellowy white, or rosé, but it's got teeth, my dear, and it loves the late night—just like *Mack the Knife*.

LANDMARK

The Jura is such a steep and frosty growing region that vignerons can prune vines in the morning and ski in the afternoon. It's only about an hour's drive to Station des Rousses, a popular alpine ski resort.

DIGGING DEEPER

Mondeuse *(MAHN-dooz)*: A plummy purple grape grown in Jura, Savoie, and Switzerland. Did you know that there is a Canton of Jura in Switzerland, by the way? *Mon dieu*! It's so confusing.

Savoie *(SAV-wah)*: Wine region south of the Jura, noted for its Mondeuse and crisp, inexpensive white blends. Even though it's spitting distance from the banking center of Geneva, these winemakers don't have the *savoir-faire* to overcharge for their bottles. Hurrah!

Trousseau *(TROO-soh)*: Yet another delightful find in the Jura's *trousseau*, this is a dark-skinned grape that's blended with Poulsard to add color. Of course, Chardonnay and Pinot Noir are also grown in the Jura, but they aren't as much fun to say.

BURGENLAND ZWEIGELT

It might sound like "burger land," but Austria's top red wine region is shaped like a chicken drumstick. Hungry Hungary takes a bite of the fleshy thigh at Burgenland. Located at the edge of Central Europe's expansive Pannonian Plain and basking in sunshine, this isn't the Alpine Austria of your preconceptions.

NEUSIEDLERSEE

AUSTRIA

BURGENLAND

GEO QUIZ

Burgenland *(BOOR-gun-land)*: You **boor**—you should get to know Burgenland! Bordering Hungary, plus a bit of Slovenia, balmy Burgenland is a landscape of wide-open steppe, encompassing a **gherkin**-shaped lake.

Neusiedlersee *(NOI-zeed-lair-zee)*: In hot Burgenland, the Zweigelt vineyards around the shores of Neusiedlersee (Lake Neusiedl) enjoy the temperature modulation of the water. The national park on the banks of the lake is a beautiful thing **to see**, but all the migratory birds here can be **noisy** at times.

KEY PLAYERS

Zweigelt *(SVY-gult)*: Bred just after World War I and dressed in black like a **spy**, Zweigelt might feel **guilt** for overtaking its mother, Blaufränkisch, as Austria's most popular red grape. But it fits with the current **zeitgeist**: It's lightweight and quaffable, while its black currant notes lend it intrigue and substance.

Blaufränkisch *(BLAU-frank-ish)*: Native to Austria, **blue-**

CULTURAL SNAPSHOT

Like Zweigelt and Blaufränkisch, eighteenth-century composer Joseph Haydn was an Austrian-born multi-national, too. Hear his music every September at the International Days of Haydn Festival at the Austro-Hungarian Esterházy Palace.

Summer at Lake Neusiedl, good for water sports and ripening grapes

skinned Blaufränksich is widespread throughout Europe under many different names, including Kékfrankos (Hungary), Blauer Limberger, and Lemberger (Germany). Those who say it's as strong as Syrah aren't being entirely *frank*—it may be spicy, but light-to-medium-bodied Lemberger is more suited to a *lentil burger* than a steak.

LANDMARK

Burgenland gets the hottest weather in Austria, with warm temperatures lasting long into autumn. Visitors cool off by jumping into Lake Neusiedl.

DIGGING DEEPER

Portugieser *(POOR-too-GFE-zur)*: *Portuguese*-born but Austrian-raised, this red grape is popular in Austria, Germany, Hungary, and Romania. It makes an inexpensive, plummy red wine that tastes good chilled. It's not *poor to gaze at,* though, thanks to its deep purple color.

Spätburgunder/Blauburgunder *(SHPAIT-boor-GUN-der/BLAU-boor-GUN-der)*: *Burgundian* Pinot Noir is called Spätburgunder in Germany, where it's extremely popular; in Austria, it's Blauburgunder. The Teutonic take on this grape might be a *shade* lighter than most, but if you spill it on your *blouse*, it won't leave such a bad *stain.*

CENTRAL OTAGO PINOT NOIR

What's red on the bottom and white on the top? Santa Claus, the Polish flag, and … the South Island of New Zealand. It might be top-heavy with Sauvignon Blanc, but down south, Central Otago (oh-TAH-goh) is all about Pinot Noir.

NEW ZEALAND

—— CENTRAL OTAGO

TOP TERMS

Bannockburn *(BAA-nuhk-BUHN or BURN)*: Pack your **Ban** antiperspirant if you plan to visit Central Otago's best-known sub-zone in the summer, when it gets **burning**-hot summer days.

Pinot Noir *(PEE-noh NWAHR)*: Compared with the rest of Central Otago, the stripped land around Bannockburn looks as dry and brown as a **peanut** shell. Somehow, this landscape yeilds dark, smoky, soul-**piercing** Pinot Noir.

GEO QUIZ

Gibbston: The verdant, chilly, high-elevation Gibbston Valley, west of Bannockburn, is another sub-zone of Central Otago. It turns out pretty Pinots fragrant with raspberries. If it were a **Gilbert and Sullivan** Pandora radio station, it would play "I'm called Little Buttercup," and "The Flowers that Bloom in the Spring."

Canterbury: Central Otago's northern neighbor produces floral, earthy Pinots, which are as intricate and long on the finish as an original edition of

CULTURAL SNAPSHOT

Central Otago's Scottish community has so influenced NZ culture that there's a term for a NZ rugger who plays for Scotland: a "Kilted Kiwi." Which is why you should sip Central Otago Pinot *Noir* while watching the All *Blacks* play Scotland.

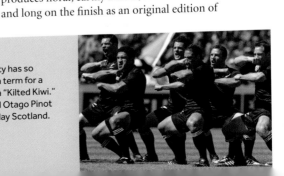

"How does Pinot grow here? How did I get up here?"

The Canterbury Tales. The Waipara Valley *(WYE-prah)* sub-region is particularly admired.

LANDMARK

The land around former mining town Bannockburn was so stripped by nineteenth-century gold miners that it looks like the Arizona desert. Strangely, this altered landscape has emerged as unparalleled for growing Pinot Noir. To get a view of the moonscape, ride a mountain bike up Duffer's Saddle, the highest road in the nation, and look northeast.

DIGGING DEEPER

Marlborough *(MAHRL-bruh)*: The northernmost region of the South Island might be famous for its *marble*-white Sauvignon Blanc, but it produces Pinot, as well. It may not be as unique as the Pinot from Central Otago, but it's herbaceous and brambly.

Wairarapa *(WYE-rah-RAH-pah)*: If you are wondering *why* Pinot Noir is classified here as a "Light Red," and can't *wrap* your mind around a red wine style that isn't rich, check out the bolder Pinots from Wairarapa, with their sweet, ripe fruit notes. This well-known sub-zone of Martinborough (not to be confused with Marlborough) can be found in the southernmost divet of the North Island, near the city of Wellington.

GETTING THE SUB-REGIONS STRAIGHT

If your head is spinning from what you just read, it's not just the New Zealand Pinot talking. To review, here's a quick list of New Zealand's key Pinot Noir regions and their well-known sub-zones, listed in order from north to south:

NORTH ISLAND

Martinborough, sub-region: Wairarapa.

SOUTH ISLAND

Central Otago, sub-regions: Bannockburn, Gibbston.
Canterbury, sub-region: Waipara Valley.
Marlborough, sub-regions: don't worry about it ... just drink more Pinot Noir.

WASHINGTON RED BLEND

The city of Seattle might be gray and drizzly, but most of Washington's wine grapes are grown on the east side of the state, in the rain shadow of the Cascade Mountains. The summers are hot and dry, and the grapes are fiercely flavorful. Cab, Merlot, and Syrah can be leathery and tough, yet soft around the edges.

UNITED STATES

WASHINGTON

COLUMBIA VALLEY
YAKIMA VALLEY

TOP TERMS

Columbia Valley: Like a map of **Christopher Columbus's** travels, the Columbia Valley wine region feels like it covers half the planet. In fact, this catch-all wine region covers 11,000,000 acres, or one-third of Washington State.

Yakima (*YAAK-ih-MAH*) Valley: The high-desert steppes, summer heat, and fast-draining silt-loam soils of the Columbia Valley's largest and oldest sub-region wouldn't even look welcoming to a **yak**, but they do appeal to Cabernet Sauvignon and Merlot.

KEY PLAYERS

Cabernet Sauvignon (*KAB-air-nay SOH-vin-YOHN*): Washington Cabs balance immense power and sumptuous dark-chocolate-and-cherry flavor with an underlying leanness. Their woody aromas carry you back to the **cabins** of high-plains homesteaders.

Merlot (*MAIR-loh*): Blueberries, plums, cocoa powder, a **marrow**-like richness and the sweet pitch of heady

CULTURAL SNAPSHOT
The arid steppes of eastern Washington and Oregon are rodeo country. The standard lineup includes wild cow milking, calf roping, steer wrestling, and crazy young cowboys risking their lives on bucking broncos and angry bulls' backs.

Washington wine country snapshot: a few farms, plenty of wild frontier

alcohol are countered by perky acidity in Washington Merlot, making this a red wine you just want to **wallow** in … or blend with Cabernet Sauvignon.

LANDMARK

Eastern Washington is a rugged place with long stretches of open road and plenty of public land where visitors can roam. This is frontier country, fragrant with the scent of sagebrush and wild juniper bushes—aromas you'll also find in a glass of Washington Cabernet Sauvignon.

DON'T STOP THERE

Syrah *(SEE-rhah; sih-RAH)*: This spicy, peppery Rhône Valley red is a rising star in Washington, where it is often blended with Grenache and Mourvèdre. With fire-**seared raw** meat, pine needles, rosemary, black olives, and balsamic vinegar, it can be as satisfying as a full meal.

Walla Walla *(WAHL-ah WAHL-ah)*: There are no **walls** between the **two** states of Washington and Oregon, and this appellation stretches across the eastern reaches of both. Its fast-draining soils and sweeping hillsides add up to outstanding Syrah, Cab, and Merlot.

Cabernet Franc *(KAB-air-nay FRAHN)*: To be **frank**, a new crop of restrained, herbaceous wines made in a Loire Valley style signal that Cab Franc may be the grape to watch.

EXTRA CREDIT

MORE COLUMBIA VALLEY SUB-ZONES TO KNOW

Horse Heaven Hills: Is nearly as large and prolific as its northern neighbor, the Yakima Valley. *Wild horses* surely once roamed these *heavenly* slopes and looked across the Columbia River to what is now the state of Oregon.

Yakima Valley: *Severus Snape* or *Wesley Snipes*—take your pick— stands atop a *red mountain, trying to herd yaks while rattlesnakes* hiss at his feet. And that covers the Yakima Valley's sub-zones, **Rattlesnake Hills**, **Red Mountain**, and **Snipes Mountain**.

Ancient Lakes, Lake Chelan *(shuh-LAAN)*, **Naches** *(NAH-chez)* **Heights, Wahluke** *(wahl-OOK)* **Slope**: *Ancient nachos shellacked with cheese would look nasty in* these northern sub-appellations, wouldn't they?

NAPA VALLEY RED BLEND

The USA's best-known wine region is the small-but-mighty Napa Valley. Just north of San Francisco and about an hour inland from the California coast, it tilts westward at its top, echoing the shape of the state. The pleasant Mediterranean climate here is ideal for grape-growing as well as for visiting.

UNITED STATES

NAPA VALLEY

CALIFORNIA

GEO QUIZ

Napa Valley: The drive from the city of Napa to the valley's northernmost town of Calistoga is almost too short to fit in a *nap*, but it packs in lots of sub-appellations. However, unlike in Europe, where more specific place names are a sign of quality, many wineries prefer to print the general "Napa Valley" name on their labels due to its *international* recognition.
Oakville: The balmy Oakville sub-zone marks the center point of the valley. You can bet your bottom dollar that the world-famous wineries here invest a lot in new *oak* barrels for their Cabernet Sauvignon.

KEY PLAYERS

Cabernet Sauvignon *(KAB-air-nay SOH-vin-YOHN)*: The big kahuna of California loves the Napa Valley's gravelly soils and soaks up the smoke of new-oak barrels. Top Napa Cabs are so black and thick with tannins that those with delicate palates might find them unbearable, so give them some *air before serving*.

CULTURAL SNAPSHOT

Traffic moves at a slow crawl on weekends, so it might be tempting to tour Napa by limo. But most quality wineries, fed up with groups of tipsy tourists, have banned big cars. Show you're serious by designating a driver and using the spit buckets.

Oh so Napa: a faux thirteenth-century Tuscan castle

Meritage *(MAIR-ih-tihj)*: To protect the **heritage** of Bordeaux, France, where Cabernet-based red blends originated, some wine labels are printed with the American term "Meritage" (a mashup of **Merlot** and **heritage)** instead of "Bordeaux blend."

LANDMARK

In the Napa Valley, the architecture is like the wine—the general consensus being, the bigger, the better. There's a magnificent Persian temple, a hilltop tasting room accessed by a private aerial tram, and a thirteenth-century Tuscan castle. Bang-for-your-buck tasting tip: Seek out the small, family-owned estates, and the earnest vintners toiling away in modest warehouses and barns.

DIGGING DEEPER

Merlot *(MAIR-loh)*: Velvety, chocolatey Merlot is the second grape of the Napa Valley. It's often blended with Cabernet Sauvignon, as it is in Bordeaux, France, to bring notes of **mellow** mocha to the leathery tobacco character of Cab.

Chardonnay *(SHAHR-doh-NAY)*: It's not a red grape, but we can't talk Napa without mentioning Chard. The standard Napa Valley style is a love-it-or-hate-it confection of butterscotch, caramel, and smoke, with a texture that is as soft as a **Shar Pei** puppy's coat.

EXTRA CREDIT

MORE TOP CAB SUB-ZONES, NORTH TO SOUTH

Calistoga: Just as you can ski and surf on a single day in **California**, Calistoga is noted for its highs and lows, in temperature and elevation.

Howell Mountain: Drink too much of this ultra-ripe red and you'll be **howling** like a wolf.

Spring Mountain: Nights as cold as a **mountain spring** capture fresh flavors on these slopes.

St Helena *(hell-EE-nah)*: Hotter temps at a lower elevation make for a **helluva** rich red wine.

Rutherford: The **ruddy** soil gives the wines a cocoa-powder-like, dusty mouthfeel.

Atlas Peak: Unlike **Atlas**, who held up the world, these mountaintop wines are leaner.

Stags Leap: Crumbly soils and rocky outcroppings create reds as soft as a deer's coat but as powerful as a **leaping stag**.

Yountville: They aren't any higher than an **anthill**, but these valley-floor vineyards build rich baked-fig notes into Cabernets.

Mount Veeder: Somewhat higher-elevation vineyards grow fruit with **leaner**, briary flavors.

SONOMA COUNTY ZINFANDEL

Coastal Sonoma County runs north to south, pointing down at San Francisco like an arrow. Despite its waterfront address, inland Sonoma gets just as hot as the neighboring Napa Valley, making this region prime for bold red wine grape-growing.

UNITED STATES

SONOMA COUNTY

CALIFORNIA

TOP TERMS

Zinfandel: Forget about the saccharine, pink "White Zin" your great aunt keeps in the fridge. Bold red Zinfandel is the same grape as southern Italy's rustic Primitivo. The wine has the *zing* of high alcohol, but its irresistible spiced-blackberry-jam flavors counteract any burning *Zippo* lighter-fluid effect.

Dry Creek Valley: This tiny sub-zone north of the town of Healdsburg is a leader in Zinfandel. It's not really that *dry*, though. Between the Russian River, Dry Creek, Lake Sonoma, and numerous small ponds, there's plenty of fog, water—and wine—to go around.

GEO QUIZ

Sonoma Valley: Within the larger county of the same name, this southern *valley* appellation gets cooling winds but is sheltered by the Sonoma Mountains, *so normally* it stays dry when wet weather comes in from the coast.

Russian River Valley: It's not exactly the *Russian tundra*, but bring a jacket when you visit this sub-zone, as it's

CULTURAL SNAPSHOT

Spicy, sweet, sticky, and impossible to have just one taste of, all-American barbecue sauce has a lot in common with Zinfandel. So fire up the grill and slather some sauce on those ribs the next time you're itching to open a bottle of Zinfandel.

Winemaking in the Wild West? Why not?

known for its chilly evening fogs. Hot days make for ripe flavors while those cold nights pack in juicy acidity.

LANDMARK

Zinfandel was planted in Sonoma County as far back as the 1850s. To get a sense of what life was like for Gold Rush vinetenders, visit Jack London State Historic Park, the former home of the swashbuckling adventurer-author. This homesteader-era ranch includes an old distillery, Sherry barn, and winery—proof that Sonomans have always taken their beverages seriously.

DIGGING DEEPER

Alexander Valley: Warm, with gravelly soils, this Sonoma sub-zone turns out Zinfandel that tastes like your Aunt *Alexandra's* blackberry crumble.

Paso Robles *(PAAS-oh ROH-blez)*: Adios, Sonoma Valley; it's time to head south on a ***road trip past*** the Los Padres National Forest. Massive "Paso," as it's colloquially known, is down in San Luis Obispo County, where there is another concentration of old Zinfandel vines.

PASO ROBLES SYRAH BLEND

UNITED STATES

CALIFORNIA

PASO ROBLES

Paso Robles (PAAS-oh ROH-blez) *overlooks the Pacific Ocean from the foothills of California's Santa Lucia Coastal Mountain Range. Its gently rolling slopes, semi-arid climate, and crumbly soils grow sensational Syrah.*

TOP TERMS

Paso Robles: This large, *pastoral,* sun-*roasted*, wind-blown wine region is parceled up into eleven sub-zones that *pass many roads,* with a wide variety of soil types that accommodate numerous grape varieties. It's California's capital of Rhône-style red wines.

Santa Barbara County: South of Paso and just north of the *sandy* beaches of the town of Santa Barbara is another Syrah hotspot. Rhône-style grapes are particularly abundant in the prominent sub-regions of the Santa Ynez *(ee-NEZ)* Valley and the Sta Rita Hills. So think of Syrah going to visit his ***Aunt Barbara and cousins Inez and Rita***.

KEY PLAYERS

Syrah *(sih-RAH)*: Peppery, meaty, and herbaceous, with notes of olive and black currant, serious California Syrah looks to France's Rhône Valley as its model, but *que será, será:* Sometime it's just dense, plush, and all-American.

Grenache *(gruh-NASH)*/**Mourvèdre** (MOOR-ved-ruh):
Two traditional blending partners for Syrah in France's
Rhône Valley have also found homes on the ranches of
California. Exuberantly fruity, brash Grenache brightens
ashy, brooding Syrah with its perky acidity and cherry-
strawberry notes. If Syrah is **serious** and Grenache is
flashy, Mourvèdre, known as Monastrell in Spain,
moves the other two toward dark mocha and earth notes.

Olive harvest in Paso Robles

LANDMARK

Despite its Wild West history, there are spots in and
around Paso Robles that could be mistaken for France's
Southern Rhône. The climate supports lavender fields
and olive-tree groves, creating a Provençal atmosphere.
You can taste fresh, green, extra-virgin olive oil at olive
farms just as you would taste wine at a tasting room.

DIGGING DEEPER

El Dorado: It's "Over the Mountains of the Moon, down
the Valley of the Shadow," as Edgar Allan Poe put it in his
poem "Eldorado." Or, at least, it's a five-hour drive north
of Paso, nearly at Lake Tahoe. The high-**elevation, dry**
El Dorado sub-zone of the larger Sierra Foothills wine
region makes darn fine Rhône-style wines.
Sonoma County: Both Napa and Sonoma have their fair
share of Syrah producers, but the highest concentrations
of Rhône Rangers are in Sonoma's Russian River Valley
and Dry Creek Valley sub-regions. **So no more counting**
northern California out of the Syrah set.

California has been producing wine for more than two centuries

WHITE RHÔNE & MORE

Carignan *(CAH-ree-NYAH)*:
California's Rhône obsession
doesn't stop with the traditional
trio of Grenache, Syrah, and
Mourvèdre. The red grape
Carignan is widely planted here.

Viognier *(VEE-oh-NYAY)*:
Tends toward high alcohol
and intense peach-apricot
aromas. The Paso Robles style
is downright tropical, with guava,
passion fruit, papaya, and mango
aromas. It is the most popular
variety to be bottled on its own;
the rest of the white grapes tend
to appear in white blends.

Roussanne *(ROO-san)*: Is
honeyed, rich, fragrant, and
golden in color.

**Grenache Blanc *(gruh-NASH
BLAHN)*:** Brings acidity and
apple flavors to blends.

Marsanne *(MAHR-san)*: Makes
a powerful, spicy wine.

CENTRAL VALLEY CARMÉNÈRE

The slender nation of Chile is a vertical stack of wine-producing valleys. Each dissects the nation horizontally, from the Andes Mountains to the Pacific Ocean. At the center of the stack is the aptly named Central Valley, just south of Santiago.

CHILE
CENTRAL VALLEY

TOP TERMS

Carménère *(KAHR-may-NAIR)*: ***Carmen Miranda*** left the old world (she was born in Portugal) and put on ***airs*** when she got to South America. And Carménère has all but disappeared from France but shines in Chile.

Central Valley: The ***centrally*** located Central Valley encompasses four of Chile's best-known wine producing valleys: Rapel, Maipo, Curicó, and Maule.

DIGGING DEEPER

Colchagua *(kohl-CHAH-gwah)* **Valley**: Carménère can look as black as ***coal*** and taste smoky when it comes from this sub-zone of Rapel in the foothills of the ***chalky***-white topped Andes. If you visit this sun-soaked, high-elevation wine region, be sure to stay hydrated with plenty of ***agua***.

Rapel *(rah-PELL)* **Valley**: Like an action hero ***rappelling*** down an Andean cliff then jumping into the sea, Rapel reaches all the way from the Andes Mountains to the foothills to the Chilean coast. As such, a wide variety of grapes can thrive here.

CULTURAL SNAPSHOT

Wine notes in verse form? Nobel Prize-winning Chilean poet and diplomat Pablo Neruda eloquently praised his nation's top red grape variety in his 1954 "Ode to Wine," calling it "topaz," "smooth," and "velvety."

The rustic grandeur of the Museo El Huique is like a fine Carménère

LANDMARK

Carménère resonates with everyone on the socio-economic spectrum, and so do the museums of the Colchagua Valley. The cultural heritage collection at Museo Colchagua tells the story of all the people of Chile. For these folks, there's plenty of inexpensive Chilean Carménère in the ten-buck range to choose from. The region's other notable museum, Museo San José del Carmen de el Huique, is the preserved 2,600-acre estate of nineteenth-century landed gentry. Their descendants must be the ones buying those fancy Carménères that cost more than $100 a pop.

OTHER OPTIONS

Cabernet Sauvignon *(KAB-air-nay SOH-vin-YOHN)*: Colchagua Valley has been called "the **Napa Valley** of Chile," so it should come as no surprise that Cab Sauv is the most planted grape here. Think of Coalchagua, and you might think of smoky, charcoaly Cabernet, which just happens to rhyme with **charcoal gray**.

Merlot *(MAIR-loh)*: Mild, velvety Merlot, along with spicy Carménère, is often **merged** with Cab Sauv in red blends to **mellow** Cabernet's bold tobacco notes, which might bring to mind the **Marlboro** man—or, in the Colchagua Valley, he'd be called the Marlboro **huaso** (that's Colchaguan for "cowboy").

EXTRA CREDIT

OUTSIDE COLCHAGUA VALLEY

Curicó (kur-ee-KOH) Valley: Just south of Santiago and north of the Rapel Valley, Curicó is another major producer of Cabernet Sauvignon and Carménère as well as Merlot. But with more rain and much less production than Colchagua, it is something of a *curio*.

Maipo *(MY-poh)* Valley: On page 129 you'll read about Maipú in Argentina and wonder if this is a *typo*. It is not. Maipú was named after a battle in Maipo that pitted South American rebels against Spanish royalist forces. The *mighty* rebels won. Surrounding Santiago on its western side, Maipo is drier than Rapel, notable for its long history and *mighty* Cabernet Sauvignon.

MENDOZA MALBEC

MENDOZA

ARGENTINA

Argentina's wine regions follow the vertical line of the Andes. Altogether, they form the outline of a skier. Salta is the cap, Catamarca the goggles, La Rioja the scarf, San Juan the jacket, and southernmost Patagonia is a stubby ski. Powerhouse Mendoza is the skier's legs, bent at the knees, propelling the rest.

TOP TERMS

Malbec *(MAHL-beck)*: Redolent of licorice, black plum, and espresso, Malbec is such a dark shade of red that if you spill it on that stylish new ensemble from the *mall* you can't take it *back* and return it.

Mendoza *(men-DOH-zah)*: Due east of Buenos Aires, high-elevation Mendoza hugs the eastern foothills of the Andes and is Argentina's most prominent wine region. If you're thinking of clearing some of this rocky and unforgiving land to plant vines, be prepared to have to *mend your bulldozer.*

OTHER OPTIONS

Torrontés *(toh-roh-TESS)*: This white wine unleashes a *torrent* of tropical flower and fruit aromas.

Bonarda *(boh-NAHR-dah)*: Argentina's second most-planted red grape was headed for the *boneyard* before viticulturists learned to prune it back to produce less fruit, of higher quality. Nowadays, it's a plush and pleasing sipper.

CULTURAL SNAPSHOT

Gauchos are Argentine cowboys who ride the range and round up cattle by day. By night they roast steaks over open flames and drink bottles of tobacco-scented, blood-red Mendoza Malbec. Then they *doze* off for a while.

LANDMARK

At nearly 23,000 feet (7,010 meters), snow-capped, sun-soaked Aconcagua is the highest peak in the western and southern hemispheres and the pinnacle of the Andes too. Likewise, Mendoza wine country is high-altitude, making for wines that are as bold as mountain climbers.

DIGGING DEEPER

Luján de Cuyo *(loo-HAHN day KOO-yoh)*: Argentina's best-known producers—names as famous (but by no means as infamous) as that of Lindsay **Lohan**—populate Mendoza's central sub-region. In this desert-like climate, days tend to be hot and dry, while at night it **cools off**.

Maipú *(my-POO)*: If most Malbec overwhelms your delicate sensibilities, try the lighter and fruitier reds from this sub-appellation just west of Luján de Cuyo, where the vines say, "**My poo** is not as smelly as yours."

Valle de Uco *(vah-YAY day OO-koh)*: It's called a **valley**, but **au contraire**, this westerly portion of Mendoza abuts the Andes and sits high above its viticultural neighbors.

High-alititude Argentine vineyards: crisp clean air and direct sunlight

LEFT-BANK BORDEAUX CABERNET SAUVIGNON

From the Bay of Biscay on France's west coast, the Gironde estuary splits into the Garonne and Dordogne Rivers. The Bordeaux (BOHR-doh) wine region follows this line, with the Cabernet-loving Left Bank occupying the southwest side of this slanted fork.

FRANCE

BORDEAUX

TOP TERMS

Cabernet Sauvignon *(KAB-air-nay SOH-vin-YOHN)*: Cab rules on the Left Bank, but it's typically blended with Cabernet Franc for a spice *cabinet* of complexity and *suave* Merlot for smoothness. **Merlot** *(MAIR-loh)*: Confusingly, the Left Bank grows more Merlot than Cab Sauv. However, the top châteaux tend to favor Cab in their red blends. Cabernet Franc, Malbec, and Petit Verdot make the party even merrier.

DELVING DEEPER

First Growth/1er Cru/Premier Cru *(PRUH-meer CROO)*: In Bordeaux, the most *premier*, *crucial* châteaux are ranked by importance, which seems almost *cruel*. The so-called First Growth, or Premier Cru, is written "1er" as shorthand on many wine lists. Today the rankings are not as important as they once were and any of the "classified growths" (First through Fifth) is considered to be a great châteaux.

CULTURAL SNAPSHOT

Bordeaux sometimes *borders* on the absurd—top wines are rated prior to release and sold as futures for thousands of dollars. Fortunately, however, if you're short on *dough*, this diverse region also offers plenty of bargains.

Miroir d'Eau, on the Garonne River, is the world's largest reflecting pool

Haut Médoc *(OH may-DUHK)*: The Médoc sub-region occupies the western half of the Left Bank **bloc**. Haut Médoc, just south, is home to the fashionable **haute** châteaux that use so much expensive new-barrel **oak** that you could build a **dock** out of them.

LANDMARK

The Miroir d'Eau on Bordeaux's grandiose Place de la Bourse is the world's largest reflecting pool. Periodically, it turns into a misting fountain, making it a popular summer escape for families. It's symbolic of the Left Bank wine regions: The wines range from regal to plebeian, the vineyards face the water, and underlying everything is a layer of gray rock.

DIGGING DEEPER

Bordeaux Blanc *(BLAH)*: A **blonde** blend of mostly Sémillon and Sauvignon Blanc, Bordeaux Blanc can either be inexpensive, light, citrusy, and floral or else silky, spicy (and more expensive), like a lemon-ginger mousse. Its two personalities might be likened to those of two famous blondes … say, fun and perky Kate Hudson and serious, deep Cate Blanchett.

Graves *(GRAHV)*: The southern section of the Left Bank, Graves is known for its **gravelly** soils, which make for minerally white and red wines.

RIGHT-BANK BORDEAUX MERLOT

Debonair Bordeaux grips western France like a hand on a dancer's waist. On closer examination, it looks like the northerly Right Bank—along with neighboring Entre-Deux-Mers—is the thumb and fingers, reaching out to grasp a glass of wine.

FRANCE

BORDEAUX

TOP TERMS

Pomerol *(POH-muh-rholl)*: Along with St-Émilion, Pomerol is one of the two top appellations of the Right Bank. Like a **Pomeranian**, Pomerol is tiny. And its Merlots are as plush and luxuriant as that gorgeous fluffy fur.

Merlot *(MAIR-loh)*: The top Right Bank estates treat their soft Merlot grapes gently, making for a wine as elegant as the sort of lady you might see leaving her *château* with her Pomeranian.

OTHER OPTIONS

Cabernet Sauvignon *(KAB-air-nay SOH-vin-YOHN)*: The favorite grape of the best Left Bank châteaux, Cab is the sinewy counterpart to soft Merlot. A Cab-based blend that includes a minority of Merlot is like Marilyn **Monroe** in a taxi *cab*: Voluptuous opulence surrounded by a framework of solid steel.

Cabernet Franc *(KAB-air-nay FRAHN)*: The third grape of Bordeaux plays a prominent part in many Right Bank

CULTURAL SNAPSHOT

Left Bank, Right Bank: Which is which? Picture two banks that deal in wine instead of money. The Cabernet Bank is on the left side of the street and the Merlot Bank is on the right. "C" comes before "M", so you can remember the order alphabetically.

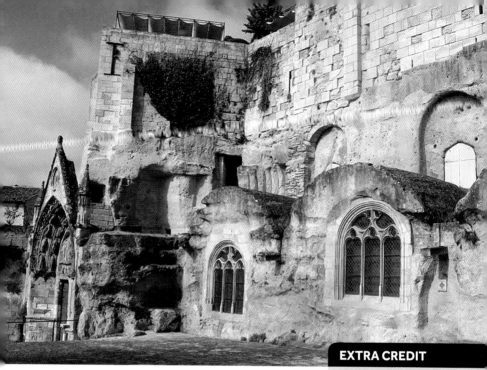

St-Émilion boasts a church carved out of a massive hunk of limestone

reds. It adds herbaceous and spicy notes to Bordeaux blends; think of it as the spice *cabinet* of the region.

LANDMARK

In the picturesque hilltop town of St-Émilion, just south of Pomerol, is the Monolithic Church, a cathedral carved out of a single hunk of limestone. In addition to the requisite soaring arches over the nave there are underground catacombs, also carved from the same piece of rock. Cool and damp, they'd be the ideal place for storing the delicate Merlots of St-Émilion and Pomerol.

DIGGING DEEPER

Entre-Deux-Mers *(ON-truh duh MAIR)*: The land that's not "between two seas" (as the French would suggest) but between two rivers—Dordogne (north) and Garonne (south). Look here for value-priced reds and dry whites. While Right- or Left-Bank Bordeaux may belong in a white-tablecloth restaurant, it's entirely fine to park a glass of Entre-Deux-Mers *on a tray* next to your easy *chair*.

LANGUEDOC-ROUSSILLON RED BLEND

The hungry Mediterranean takes a bite out of southern France at Languedoc (LONG-dok), while Roussillon (ROO-SEE-yohn) watches from the heights of the Pyrénées. The combined Languedoc-Roussillon is the most productive wine region in the nation.

FRANCE

LANGUEDOC ROUSSILLON

TOP TERMS

Corbières *(KOHR-bee-YAIR)*: Your old stuffed *corduroy bear* wasn't priceless until your parents put it in the donation box. And the largest sub-zone of the Languedoc, long maligned, has only recently garnered acclaim for its old-vine Carignan-based blends.

Minervois *(MEE-nayr-VWAH)*: Noted for its high-quality reds as well as intriguing whites made from historic indigenous grapes, Minervois, just north of Corbières, is the *Minerva* of the Languedoc—ancient, cerebral, and poetic.

KEY PLAYERS

Mourvèdre *(MOOR-ved-ruh)*: As black as a *mourning* coat, as *morbid* as red blood, Mourvèdre brings dark color and surly tannins to red blends.

Syrah *(SEE-rhah; sih-RAH)*: *She-Ra*, with her red cape and lethal sword, packs a punch. And so does spicy and savory Syrah, the wine that tastes like a pepper-crusted steak.

CULTURAL SNAPSHOT

Languedoc-Roussillon is distinctly Mediterranean, with a dry, warm climate, mountainous terrain, and local delicacies like wild boar and figs. Many olive trees provide for tasty tapenade, which matches the savory Languedoc reds perfectly.

Collioure, near the Spanish border, poised between forest and sea

Grenache *(gruh-NASH)*: Notable for its ripe strawberry nose, bright color, and high alcohol, Grenache brightens up a red blend like a cranberry-sauce *garnish* peps up your Thanksgiving turkey.

LANDMARK

At first glance, Collioure looks like one more historic fortified seaside town, but it is a diverse winemaking epicenter, with a colorful history, rooted to a spot where the mountains meet the sea and Spain meets France. Wines here range from white to rosé to red to Banyuls (dessert style).

GEO QUIZ

Faugères *(FOH-zhair)*: With its higher elevations, Faugères grows red grapes with fresh acidity, making for wines that are slightly more *debonair* than those of funky Corbières to the southwest.

Saint-Chinian *(SAHN shee-NYAHN)*: This sub-zone between Faugères and Minervois has *shimmied* its way into the hearts of wine lovers in recent years with its spicy, licorice-scented reds.

Roussanne *(ROO-san)*: A pink-tinged white grape variety that looks like it's blushing, Roussanne pretties up white blends with aromatics, like a bit of *rouge* applied to a pale cheek.

EXTRA CREDIT

KEY SUB-REGIONS

Cahors *(KAH-ohr)*: West of the Languedoc, the Sud Ouest, or South West, is known for its burly reds. The town of Cahors turns out an inky-black Malbec-based wine that will coat your tongue like a *kaftan*.

Madiran *(MAA-dee-RAH)*: A village where the Tannat grape makes thick, *tannic* wines.

Irouléguy *(ee-ROO-leh-ghee)*: Cabernet Franc and Tannat *rule* in this obscure Basque region, where the pitch-black wines have a certain *esprit*.

Bergerac *(BAIR-zhuh-RAAK)*: *Cyrano de Bergerac* wrote letters that another guy passed off as his own. Bergerac wines could pass as Bordeaux, and they're made from the same grapes, too.

RHÔNE RED BLEND

The Rhône Valley once occupied a geopolitical hot spot. Just west of Italy, atop Provence, beneath Beaujolais and Burgundy, it hosted a series of renegade fourteenth-century popes and anti-popes at Avignon. Today, the pope is back in Rome, but the Rhône's red wines are all about alcoholic power and piquant intrigue.

FRANCE

NORTHERN RHÔNE

SOUTHERN RHÔNE

TOP TERMS

Côtes du Rhône Villages *(KOHT doo ROHN VEE-lahzh)*: Your basic Côtes du Rhône can be as anticipatory and relatively affordable as *flying coach to Rome*. "Village" wines are higher quality. And if the name of a specific village appears, even better. It's like finding out you'll be staying at a *villa*.

Northern vs. Southern Rhône: The snooty Northern Rhône has more first-rate vineyards and a cooler climate. Grenache-focused Southern Rhône red blends are fruity and friendly, with a little bit of kick. They'd charm the heck out of a plate of Carolina barbecue with their *Southern hospitality*.

KEY PLAYERS

Grenache *(gruh-NASH)*: Like a *grin under a moustache*, Grenache is a smile-eliciting grape grown in the south (as opposed to those prickly Syrahs of the Northern Rhône). It tends to be high in alcohol and scented with ripe strawberries.

CULTURAL SNAPSHOT

The city of the *lion*—Lyon—marks the northernmost point of the Rhône and the southernmost point of Beaujolais. If either region gets to claim that mascot, it's the Rhône, where the reds can taste and smell downright feral. Grrrrr!!!

The roasted slopes of Côte-Rôtie

Mourvèdre *(MOOR-ved-ruh)*: This black grape brings *more red* color to Southern Rhône blends, as well as smoke, spice, and tannin.

Syrah *(SEE-rhah; sih-RAH)*: In the Northern Rhône, *sizzlingly* spicy Syrah holds its own—except when a dash of white **Viognier** *(VEE-oh-NYAY)* is added to enhance aromatics, like a *sachet* of *violets* to a stinky sock drawer.

LANDMARK

Côte-Rôtie translates as "roasted slope." At this top-shelf commune, vineyard rows are literally carved out of the rock in steep terraces overlooking the river, where they are roasted by the sun. These wines often have a roasted-meat aroma to them, too.

DIGGING DEEPER

Châteauneuf-du-Pape *(SHAAT-oh-NEHF doo PAHP)*: It would be tough to *shatter a bottle of pop with a Nerf* football, and it's a challenge to say the name of this famous Southern Rhône appellation, too. It can be a blend of up to thirteen different grape varieties and tends to be spicy and savory with ripe red cherry notes.

Luberon *(LOO-buh-roh)* and Ventoux *(VAHN-too)*: "*Lou, bro, hop in the van to* pick up some of these dirt-cheap, rustic table wines from the southeastern-most part of the Rhône, okay?"

PIEDMONT BAROLO

Meat eaters, take note: Lepre al civet, or bunny braised in red wine, is a local specialty of Piedmont. And the outline of the wine region of Piedmont—Piemonte (PEE-ay-MOHN-tay) in Italian—looks like a shaggy hare that's facing east. The revered sub-zones of Barolo and Barbaresco, separated by the town of Alba, are in its belly.

PIEDMONT

ITALY

TOP TERMS

Barolo *(bah-ROH-loh)*: A wine for those with plenty of patience, classic Barolo should rest in your cellar for at least a decade before you open it. It turns an unusual shade of faded red velvet (such as you might see at a *baronial* castle) over time.

Barbaresco *(BAHR-bahr-ESS-koh)*: Same grape, different neighborhood. The Barbaresco zone enjoys a milder climate and thus produces wines that are softer, spicier, and more aromatic. While both are *barbell*-big wines, you could actually sip a glass of young-ish Barbaresco at a *bar* without experiencing the urge to rush to the dentist afterward.

DIGGING DEEPER

Nebbiolo *(NEB-ee-OH-loh)*: High on acid and tannin. Aromatic with notes of tar, roses, violets, and earth. Deeply flavored like bitter dark chocolate and truffles, with an orange-peel note in the finish. In short, there's nothing *nebbish* about the most prominent red grape

CULTURAL SNAPSHOT

When in Piedmont, don't miss the chance to sip Barolo Chinato *(bah-ROH-loh kee-NAH-toh)* after dinner. This sweetly spiced red Vermouth is Barolo wine macerated with herbs and exotics like cinchona bark and a little sugar and grappa.

of Piedmont, whether it's made in the zone of Barolo, Barbaresco, or somewhere else.

Gattinara *(GAAT-ee-NAH-rah)*: Like a *gateway narcotic*, Gattinara is a lighter, drink now Nebbiolo from northern Piedmont.

LANDMARK
Piedmont's famous Langhe Hills harbor the great vineyards of Barolo and Barbaresco as well as the priceless forests where the "Alba truffle," or white truffle, grows. No visit to Piedmont is complete without a dish of white-truffle pasta accompanied by local wine.

DON'T STOP
Barbera *(bahr-BAIR-uh)*: The most prevalent red grape in Piedmont goes by its own name on wine labels, typically followed by the title of the growing zone, such as Alba, Asti, or Monferrato. On the palate, it tends to see-saw between cranberry-pomegranate perkiness and a rather *barbaric* bloody flavor.

Dolcetto *(dohl-CHET-oh)*: Named as though it were a *dulcet-toned* passing fancy, Dolcetto used to be a red grape not worthy of thought. Today, winemakers are pumping up the black-cherry concentration in their Dolcetto wines. The result can be disappointing, or a sweet *(dolce)* success, depending on the producer and your personal taste. But the wine is dry.

Fall in Piedmont

A Piedmontese truffle dog with its quarry

VALPOLICELLA AMARONE

Within northeastern Italy's Veneto region, the Valpolicella (VAHL-pohl-lee-CHELL-ah) zone is a grouping of hills just north of the city of Verona. Its shape undulates as though it is a chubby earthworm that has just drunk too much ultra-rich, earthy, tannic Amarone and is inching toward the sparkling blue waters of the Lago di Garda for refreshment.

VALPOLICELLA

ITALY

TOP TERMS

Amarone *(AH-mah-ROH-nay)*: *Amore* for many wine-lovers is this blackish-red wine that's richer and stronger than the rest. Winemakers dry their best bunches of grapes, then ferment that concentrated sugar all the way to dryness … and mega alcohol. Finally, the wine must cellar-age for at least two years prior to release. The resulting wine is a dry, potent *animal*—14%ABV at the very minimum—that can age for decades in the cellar.

Corvina *(cohr-VEE-nah)*: Like a *red Corvette,* the top red grape of the Veneto's Valpolicella sub-zone makes peppy Valpolicella table wines and virulent Amarone.

DIGGING DEEPER

Valpolicella: The region's *value* red wine, which bears the same name as the region. The *polar* opposite of Amarone, it is fragrant and light, with the tang of sour *cherries*. Be sure to buy quality bottles labeled Classico or Classico Superiore.

Ripasso *(ree-PAH-soh)*: A Valpolicella Superiore wine

CULTURAL SNAPSHOT

Beef braised in Amarone is a classic dish in the restaurants of Verona. Other traditional local delicacies, like smoke-dried chestnuts, walnuts, porcini mushrooms, truffles, and tart cherries of the Marostica hills, echo the *aromas* of Amarone.

that's had a **second pass** at soaking up color, tannin, and alcohol thanks to a second fermentation on a **repast** of dried Amarone grapes, it's the half-way point between a basic Valpolicella and an Amarone.

LANDMARK

Castelvecchio Museum's impressive red-brick facade is that of a powerful medieval Veronese fortress. But the castle was renovated, again and again, over the centuries. Most recently, modern architect Carlo Scarpa installed linear iron doorways, clean-lined concrete and stone, and massive wooden beams while leaving the layers of alterations exposed. Like a bottle of Amarone, the Castelvecchio is more interesting than ever today, thanks to careful modifications that have ensured its longevity.

DON'T STOP THERE

DOCG: Since 2010, all Amarone della Valpolicella wines have had "DOCG," or **designation of controlled and guaranteed origin**, on their labels. That is, the region and the winemaking style warrant the highest-quality rating, according to the Italian government. Ripasso, by contrast, is a "DOC" wine style—that is, the quality is not guaranteed to be quite as high.

Single-vineyard: Some pundits complain that Amarone is overproduced and the DOCG designation doesn't really mean anything. The top winemakers of the region have responded with wines made from grapes picked in **just one carefully cultivated vineyard**. Extra verbiage on the front label of an Amarone is a tip-off that you've got a single-vineyard wine, as is an inflated price tag and a release date that's five or more years after the vintage.

Corvina grapes on the vine

The Castelvecchio Museum, as seen from the Adige River

ALTO ADIGE LAGREIN

Hyphens are the bane of the amateur wine lover. Just try saying "Trentino-Alto Adige" (tren-TEE-noh AHL-toh AH-dee-jay) three times, fast. But it won't take you all day to get to know this delightful dual region. Trentino, to the south, is more entrenched in Italy, while Alto Adige, to the north, is closer to Austria.

ALTO ADIGE
TRENTINO

ITALY

TOP TERMS

Lagrein *(lahg-RINE)*: Endemic to Alto Adige, Lagrein has been around a *long time* but only recently has been celebrated by *longsighted* winemakers who bring out the best of its velvety texture, notes of plum and spice, and food-friendly acidity.

Teroldego *(teh-ROHL-day-GOH)*: Another indigenous red that's about as old as a fossilized *pterodactyl*. It reaches its full wingspan when grown on the Rotaliano plain, in Alto Adige's southern companion, Trentino.

DIGGING DEEPER

Pinot Nero *(PEE-noh NAIR-oh)*: Pinot Noir, Blauburgunder, Spätburgunder … whatever you want to call it, in Alto Adige it makes a fresh, *blackish*-dark wine, scented with violets and dark berries.

Schiava *(skee-AH-vah)*: Alto Adige's most widely planted red grape variety yields plump, thin-skinned fruit and a pale red that's like Lagrein stripped down to its *skivvies*. In German, as Vernatsch, it's a red that tastes best chilled.

CULTURAL SNAPSHOT

Most folks in Alto Adige speak German and there's even a sizable enclave of locals who converse in the Dolomitic dialect Ladin. Perhaps indigenous grape varieties like Lagrein are so alluring here because they are as unique as the people and place.

Alto Adige vineyard, in the shadow of the Dolomites

LANDMARK

The rocky cliff walls surrounding the Dolomitic valleys of Trentino and Alto Adige reflect sunlight, trapping heat like a toaster oven. The microclimates of these wine-growing regions can vary from hot to frigid, depending on where you're standing. This means one single winery can make elegant cool-climate whites and bubblies as well as robust red wines. To visualize this diversity, take an afternoon hike in the Brenta group of Dolomites, just southwest of the wineries of Alto Adige and Trentino. As the sun sets, the white rock faces turn pink, and then a glorious red, in a phenomenon called *enrosadira*.

DON'T STOP

Liguria *(lee-GOO-ree-ah)*: Coastal Liguria is hours away from Trentino-Alto Adige, but I feel it's my **legal duty** to inform you these two northerly wine regions share a reputation for soft, crowd-pleasing red wines that pair with **legumes** or seafood as easily as they do with steak.

Rossese *(roh-SEZ-ay)*: If you like Lagrein and Pinot Nero, you'll love Rossese, especially from Liguria's Dolceacqua zone. It's an endangered variety due to the difficulty of farming the low-yield old vines in Liguria's steeply terraced vineyards. So mention it to the sommelier the next time you're at a fine Italian restaurant and you'll bask in the **rosy glow** of his or her admiration.

EXTRA CREDIT

MEET TRENTINO-ALTO ADIGE'S WHITE WINES

Gewürztraminer *(gay-VOORS-trah-meen-er)*: In volume, Trentino-Alto Adige produces more white than red wine, but the grape names don't sound as Italian as Teroldego. In fact, the Germanic-sounding grape Gewürztraminer actually originated in the Alto Adige town of Termeno sulla Strada del Vino, aka Tramin an der Weinstraße, aka "Tramin on the Wine Route."

Pinot Grigio *(PEE-noh GREE-joh)*: Alto Adige's most commonly grown white grape, closely followed in popularity by Gewürztraminer, Chardonnay, Pinot Bianco (also called Weissburgunder, Sauvignon Blanc, and Müller-Thurgau). Although some of these grapes make delicate—or even flimsy—wines in other places, the Südtirol style is firm and clean, with minerality and a silky mouthfeel.

Alto Adige Bianco *(AHL-toh AH-dee-jay bee-YAWN-koh)*: A lively blend of Pinot Bianco, Chardonnay, and Pinot Grigio—on a wine list, it's likely to be a safe bet.

CHIANTI SANGIOVESE

If mainland Italy is kicking a soccer ball, Chianti (kee-AHN-tee) provides the power. Tuscany—Toscana (toh-SKAH-nah) in Italian—is the quadricep of that booted leg. Chianti country lies at its very center and at the heart of the Italian wine industry, too. It's one of forty-something Tuscan wine-growing sub-regions but far and away the most important.

TUSCANY
CHIANTI

ITALY

TOP TERMS

Chianti: The **key** to Chianti is that it's difficult to **quantify**. The old style is medium-to-light bodied, tasting pleasantly of dried leaves, balsamic vinegar, and tomato **ketchup** while modern Chianti is rich, with plums, dried cherries, tobacco, and leather.
Sangiovese *(SAN-joh-VAY-zay)*: The Chianti grape. With its firm acidity, it makes a food-friendly wine that can range from opulent to stringent. It's sometimes described as *"sappy,"* implying a syrupy woodiness.

DIGGING DEEPER

Chianti Classico *(KLAHSS-ee-koh)* **and Rùfina** *(roo-FEE-nah)*: Chianti's top two **classic** sub-zones. At their best, the wines hit a **roof** of intensity, with pronounced spicy cherry notes and robust tannins.
Superiore and Riserva *(soo-PAIR-ee-OH-ray and ree-SAIR-vah)*: These **superior**-sounding descriptors are just indications of how long the wine was **reserved** for aging prior to release. Riserva ages longer than Superiore.

CULTURAL SNAPSHOT

Back in the Middle Ages, a border dispute between Florence and Siena was decided by a half-starved black rooster. Today, wine and olive oil bottles from Chianti Classico bear the stamp of this poor creature as a sign of quality.

Nuovo Teatro dell'Opera di Firenze—a novel take on a traditional form

LANDMARK

Florence is rich in historic opera houses dating back centuries. Then there's the angular, geometric Nuovo Teatro dell'Opera di Firenze. With technologically unparalleled acoustics and a rooftop open-air amphitheater that offers panoramic city views and is always open to the public, it's a total reinterpretation of a classic genre. In short, it's symbolic of what's going on outside the city gates with Sangiovese.

DON'T STOP THERE

Brunello di Montalcino (*broo-NELL-oh dee MONT-ahl-CHEE-noh*): South of Siena in the Montalcino zone, the climate gets hotter, the grass gets ***browner,*** and Sangiovese goes by the name Brunello. Long-lived and aggressively tannic in its youth, it's a ***monumental*** wine suggestive of black olives and gravel.

Vino Nobile di Montepulciano (*VEE-noh NOH-bee-LAY dee MAHN-tuh-pool-CHAH-noh*): Montepulciano is the name of a grape grown mostly in Abruzzo. But it's also the name of a place in Tuscany that makes wine from Sangiovese. Boasting a long, ***noble*** winemaking history, it's constantly ***pulling*** on its western neighbor ***Montalcino*** in its demand for respect. Its sandy soils make for concentrated flavor, and its perfume is often described as reminiscent of tea leaves.

ABRUZZO MONTEPULCIANO

Abruzzo (ah-BROOT-zoh), on Italy's central-eastern shore, might be shaped like a balled-up fist, but its red wines aren't brutal *in the least. They do pack a punch of color and ripe fruit, but they won't pummel your palate with tough tannins.*

| ITALY | ABRUZZO |

TOP TERMS

Montepulciano *(MOHN-tuh-pool-CHAH-noh)*: Black-tinted Montepulciano looks tough. But on the palate, this red is as guileless as a painting by a ***Montessori preschooler***, with vibrant flavors of fat ripe berries and about-to-burst cherry tomatoes.

Colline Teramane *(koh-LEE-nay tair-ah-MAH-nay)*: The vineyards in these hills north of the coastal city of Pescara get the term DOCG (ie "most excellent") on their labels. By contrast, wines labeled simply Montepulciano d'Abruzzo tend to be simpler pleasures.

DIGGING DEEPER

Rosso Conero *(ROH-soh KOH-nair-OH)*: Abruzzo's northerly neighbor, Marches, makes delicious red from the Montepulciano grape, sometimes blended with Sangiovese. In Rosso Conero, the growing area surrounding Ancona, these ***reds*** can range from simple and plummy to earthy and velvety, with woodsy, Old Spice notes that would suit ***Conan the Babarian***.

CULTURAL SNAPSHOT

Abruzzo is obsessed with chili peppers. Most home-grown recipes call for the little devils or "*diavolilli.*" And in restaurants, in place of the salt and pepper shakers, you'll find a fresh red or green chili and a pair of scissors.

Don't confuse Montepulciano, the Tuscan town, with Montepulciano, the Abruzzo grape

LANDMARK

The next time you're in Italy, say, driving a red Ferrari, point it straight for Abruzzo. This untamed region is home to three national parks and its diversity of wildlife makes it a European treasure. Revel in the unspoiled mountain roads that wind through the massive Parco Nazionale d'Abruzzo, Lazio e Molise, then cruise down through Montepulciano vineyards to the stunning Adriatic coastline. Finish your driving excursion with a glass of Montepulciano d'Abruzzo to match your peppy red car.

DON'T STOP

Molise *(moh-LEEZ-ay)*: We don't hear much about this region southwest of Abruzzo, because it's as small and quiet as a *mouse* in comparison with the rest of Italy. Most of the wines are produced by cooperatives, so they tend to be quite inexpensive. Montepulciano is the top red grape here.

Vino Nobile di Montepulciano *(VEE-noh NOH-bee-LAY dee MOHN-tuh-pool-CHAH-noh)*: This very fine Tuscan red wine is made from Sangiovese grapes, not Montepulciano grapes. It just happens to come from a town called Montepulciano. So if you see those words on a label, remember "Nobile" signifies that in *no way* are there any Montepulciano grapes in the bottle.

PUGLIA PRIMITIVO

The heel of the Italian boot, Puglia (POOL-yee-ah; also known as Apulia) looks as though it is being pulled into the Adriatic. But along with neighboring Campania and Basilicata, and more southerly Calabria and Sicily, it's pushing a rapid expansion of the southern Italian wine industry by reviving archaic grape varieties and pumping up quality.

TOP TERMS

Primitivo *(pree-mee-TEE-voh)*: In the USA, it goes by the name of Zinfandel making a blackberry syrup-like wine. In the *primitive* landscape of arid Puglia, Primitivo is more blunt and elemental, tasting of bitter coffee.

Manduria *(mahn-DOO-ree-ah)*: Discerning producers get spicy, gamey, smoked-licorice flavors from Primitivo grapes grown in the iron-rich soils around Manduria, half-way between the cities of Lecce and Taranto, which is nowhere near **Manchuria**.

DIGGING DEEPER

Negroamaro *(NAY-groh-ah-MAH-roh)*: "Amaro" might sound like *amore*, but the name of Puglia's other prominent red actually translates as "black and bitter." It has spicy, savory notes, too, and is at its best in the Salento sub-region, in particular the town of Salice Salentino.

Aglianico *(AH-lee-AH-nee-koh)*: Another of southern Italy's archaic red grapes, recently revived to great acclaim, Aglianico turns out brawny reds that would

These ancient Puglian farming huts are called trulli, truly

appeal to a gangster like **Al Capone** with its notes
of tobacco and volcanic ash. It grows in the Taurasi
zone of Campania and in the Vulture zone of Basilicata.

LANDMARK

Attenzione, archaeology buffs: If you like to see
a good-looking rock, Puglia is the place for you.
The Salento region alone boasts eighty of Italy's
one hundred known menhir sites. You can get a view
of the lack of action in the hamlet of Giurdignano,
known by locals as "the Megalithic garden" due to its
abundance of menhirs and dolmens. It's no wonder
the local grape was named "Primitivo."

DON'T STOP

Nero d'Avola *(NAIR-oh DAHV-oh-la)*: The
ubiquitous red (well, actually, black) grape of Sicily
can range from a rather *narrow*, quaffable supermarket
wine to a hedonistic *avalanche* of opulent flavors like
toasted pistachio, black currant, and cocoa.

Frappato *(frah-PAH-toh)*: Juicy Frappato can taste
(deliciously) like a strawberry-cherry *frappe* on its
own, so it tends to be blended with Nero d'Avola
for the sake of dignity. However, more serious
interpretations by top Sicilian producers have
been compared to Pinot Noir.

EXTRA CREDIT

THE OUTER EDGES OF SOUTHERN ITALIAN RED

Lacryma Christi *(lah-KREE-mah KREE-stee)*: If you're
exploring the reds of southern
Italy, sooner or later you'll meet
Lacryma Christi del Vesuvio,
which translates as—I kid you
not—"The tears of Christ." No,
this is no *laughing* matter. Here's
the *creation* myth: Nazareth's
most popular guy made a guest
appearance on Mount Vesuvius,
where he cried over Lucifer's fall
from Heaven, and somehow, that
turned to wine. Don't ask ... just
drink. The red Lacryma Christi
(there is also a white) is made
from the ancient native grapes
Piedrirosso and Sciascinoso.

Cannonau di Sardegna *(kah-noh-NOW dee sahr-DAY-nyah)*:
You could shoot a *cannon* from
Calabria and hit Sicily. *Sardinia*,
unfortunately, often gets left
off the vinous radar due to
its distance from mainland
Italy. Known as Grenache or
Garnacha in the rest of the
world, Cannonau is the earthy
red grape of this island. Often
blended with Carignan (or
Carignano), it makes a robust
wine redolent of cherries, plums,
and spices.

DOURO RED BLEND

Portugal's Douro River zone is best-known for its fortified wines, called Port. But the same grapes, from the same region, also make some of the nation's finest dry red table wines. The Dão (DOW) and Alentejo (AH-len-TAY-zhoh) make similar wines from the same grapes. Together, you can remember these three regions because your DAD would enjoy these reds.

DOURO
DÃO
PORTUGAL
ALENTEJO

TOP TERMS

Field Blend: Dozens of different grape varieties once grew together willy-nilly. They were **blended in the field** as a sort of insurance policy, since they ripened at different times. The dry reds of the Douro continue to be blends of many varieties—but today, they're mixed by the winemaker more often than by nature.

Touriga Nacional *(too-REE-gah NAH-see-oh-NAHL)*: This grape brings a **tornado** of spicy, savory, licorice flavor to Douro red blends.

Touriga Franca *(too-REE-gah FRAN-kah)*: The most-planted grape in the Douro, Franca is less forward than Nacional, with a floral, fresh-berry scent that's like **French** perfume.

MORE KEY PLAYERS

Tinta Roriz *(TEEN-tah ROH-reezh)*: Known as Tempranillo in Spain, Roriz is prized for its black color, early ripening, and tough, thick skins. It brings a dark **ruddy tint** to blends.

CULTURAL SNAPSHOT

Small quintas (estates), like da Pacheca, can now bottle and sell their own wines; formerly they were required to sell their grapes to the larger Port houses. This has contributed to the recent rapid growth of dry table wines in the Douro.

Santuário de Nossa Senhora dos Remédios—quite a climb!

Tinto Cão *(TEEN-toh KOW)*: It might sound like *tipping cows*, but it smells like a red rose, and brings thorny tannins and a velvety *cowhide* texture to blends.

LANDMARK
Duro is the Portuguese term for "tough." And working in the vineyards of the Douro is not for the weak. Unfortunately, those laborers who trek to the Santuário de Nossa Senhora dos Remédios in search of respite don't get it because there are six hundred eighty six steps to climb just to get to the front door.

GEO QUIZ
Alentejo: This *elephantine* wine region covers hot, dry southeast Portugal. Its dark red blends are dominated by Tinto Roriz, which is called Aragonez here just to *antagonize* you. They're redolent of blackberries, dark chocolate, and tar.
Dão: Just south of the Douro and centered over the Dão River. This slightly *dowdy* bucolic region's best reds are similar to those of the Douro in grape make-up, but thanks to higher elevations and a damper climate, they're more subtle, with zippy acidity and tingling white pepper notes. Which makes them excellent for pairing with *chow*.

CATALONIA GARNACHA

Bleeding-heart shaped Catalonia—Catalunya (KAT-ah-LOON-yah) in Catalan—is home to Catalan separatists, as well as some delicious blood-red wines made from the Garnacha grape. Occupying the far northeastern corner of the nation, it is anchored by the city of Barcelona.

CATALONIA

BARCELONA

SPAIN

KEY PLAYERS

Garnacha *(gahr-NAH-chah)*: Even though it's a star in France's Rhône Valley, where it's called Grenache, the Garnacha grape was born in Spain. It can make a ***gargantuan***, heady wine, sweetened by notes of strawberry and blueberry preserves.

Cariñena *(KAH-rih-NYEH-nah)*: Also native to Spain, and better-known in French (Carignan), this grape acts like Garnacha's ***caregiver***. Added to a barrel of Garnacha-based red, it props up its partner's big, gobby, fruity body with a framework of tannin and acidity.

GEO QUIZ

Priorat *(PREE-oh-RAHT)*: This small but ***preeminent*** Catalonia sub-zone is surrounded by the Montsant and Tarragona zones like the jam in the middle of a jelly donut. It's bakery-oven hot here, the parched soil is sprinkled with slate and quartz, and old Garnacha vines make blackberry cordial-like wines.

CULTURAL SNAPSHOT

In *Homage to Catalonia*, George Orwell scorns a Catalan anise liqueur called Anís del Mono, named after the monkey or *mono* that lived in the distillery. Ironically, the very best Garnachas often have an aniseed or licorice flavor to them.

Priorat and Montsant's tough vines are rugged and full of character

Montsant *(mohn-SAANT)*/**Tarragona** *(tahr-ah-GOH-nah)*/**Terra Alta** *(TEHR-ah AHL-tah)*: High-*altitude* Priorat represents the pinnacle, but its outer *moats* of Montsant and Tarragona, and neighboring Terra Alta, produce wines that are nearly as good, with that licorice-like *tarragon* flavor at the finish, for a lower *tariff*.

LANDMARK

The village of Siurana is more popular with rock climbers than it is with wine drinkers. Its vertical drops are legendary with mountaineers—in particular, "La Rambla," an ascent that has only been completed by ten climbers.

DIGGING DEEPER

Aragón *(ah-rah-GOHN)*: An alternate name for the Garnacha grape, as well as the name of a growing region inland from Catalonia that's home to a sub-zone called Cariñena. So, wouldn't you know it, Garnacha and Cariñena are grown here. These wines are not for the *arrogant*; they're *affordable alternatives* to premium Priorat.

Campo de Borja *(KAAM-poh deh BOHR-hah)*/**Calatayud** *(KAHL-ah-tah-YOOD)*: Key Aragon sub-zones. They produce a whole *catalog* of red blends, from cheapies for *campers* to *boorishly* high in alcohol and exorbitantly overpriced.

RIOJA TEMPRANILLO BLEND

RIOJA

SPAIN

In north-central Spain, the Rioja (ree-OH-hah) wine region follows the Ebro River, looking like a fiesty bull about to toss a bear rug off its back. Whether you prefer a torrid powerhouse or a cozy fireside companion, there's a Rioja red wine for you.

GEO QUIZ

Rioja Alta/Alavesa/Baja *(AHL-tah/AH-lah-BEH-sah/BAH-hah)*: The two "A" sub-zones occupy Rioja's west sides. Higher-*altitude* and cooler, they make intricate, attention-grabbing wines, like a bull performing an *Alvin Ailey* dance. Rioja Baja, the eastern "B" side, specializes in simpler wines with less intellectual *baggage*.

Ribera del Duero *(ree-BEH-ah del DWAIR-oh)*: On the opposite side of the Sierra de la Demanda range, Ribera del Duero may be a sub-zone of the Castilla y León (*kah-STEE-yah ee leh-OHN*) region, but it's the soul mate of Rioja. Its Tempranillo blends are status symbols, like the military *ribbons you wear* if you're top-rank.

KEY PLAYERS

Tempranillo *(TEM-prah-NEE-yoh)*: This red grape will stimulate your *temporal* lobes with its dried-berry flavors *tempered* by savory leather, tobacco, and paprika notes. It *needs* oak, taking on vanilla, chocolate, and cinnamon qualities depending on the type of barrel.

CULTURAL SNAPSHOT

The Vivanco Museum of Wine Culture, in Briones, exhibits a collection of artifacts, documents, and artworks spanning eight thousand years of wine history. The adjoining "Garden of Bacchus" grows more than two hundred and twenty grape varieties.

Garnacha *(gahr-NAH-chah)*: An important blending partner in Rioja and Ribera del Duero, bringing gorgeous *garnet* color and *gargantuan* ripe red-cherry and strawberry notes to cerebral Tempranillo.

LANDMARK

Urban warehouse wineries may be all the rage right now, but some of Rioja's most prominent bodegas have been located at Haro's Barrio de La Estación (railway station quarter) since the late nineteenth century, when a destructive aphid called phylloxera wiped out nearly half the vineyards in France. The French shipped barrels of Spanish wines north from these trackside warehouses and sent their expertise south. And it wasn't just winemaking expertise: One bodega in the Barrio de La Estación boasts a barrel room designed by Alexandre-Gustave Eiffel, of Eiffel Tower fame.

Railway station or Rioja winery?

DIGGING DEEPER

Castilla-La Mancha *(kah-STEE-yah lah MAHN-chah)*: This central state, south of Madrid, is a major producer of Tempranillo, most notably from the desert-like La Mancha, and the southerly sub-zone of Valdepeñas *(VAHL-deh-PEY-nyahss)*. For the most part, these are bargain-bin wines, not suitable as a gift the next time you stay at a *castle or mansion*.

Toro *(TOH-roh)*: *Bullish* sub-zone of Castilla y León, the state northwest of Castilla-La Mancha that's making a name for itself with fierce, massive red wines.

Barrel room par excellence, designed by Alexandre-Gustave Eiffel

MURCIA MONASTRELL

SPAIN

MURCIA

The southeastern Spanish coast, across the Mediterranean from Algeria, is known as the Levante. The bell-shaped state of Murcia (MOOR-see-ah) is the center of this hotbed of wine production. Long dismissed by serious wine enthusiasts, Murcia is ringing a bell for its corner of Spain these days with its knock-out reds.

GEO QUIZ

Jumilla *(hoo-MEE-yah)*: The sun-baked plateaux of Jumilla don't look promising for growing wine grapes. But despite the lack of *humidity,* they coax layers of flavor from Monastrell. And most of these wines won't *humiliate* budget-conscious shoppers.

Yecla/Bullas *(YEH-klah/BU-yahss)*: Jumilla's northern neighbor, Yecla, is high desert—no *yacht clubs* here, but with a slightly more forgiving Mediterranean climate. The southerly Bullas wine-growing zone, on the other hand, has soils that look like the surface of Mars. The grapes that make it in this inhospitable environment turn into big *bullies* when they're vinified.

KEY PLAYERS

Monastrell *(MOH-nah-STRELL)*: Better known by its French name, Mourvèdre, Monastrell is far more prolific in its native Spain. It makes full-bodied, big-fruited wines, weighty with alcohol. The best are *moderated* by acidity and meaty, olive, tomato, herb, and orange flavors.

CULTURAL SNAPSHOT

To match a Jumilla Monastrell, cook up a humble, stick-to-your-ribs *migas.* As traditionally prepared in Murcia, this dish is a simple flour-and-water dough, pan-fried to make loose dumplings. Serve with pork, a fried egg, or sardines.

Southeastern Spain's vinetenders contend with unforgiving conditions

Bobal *(boh-BAHL)***:** Its reputation may be that of a *boring* supermarket ***box***-wine grape but this native Spanish grape, widely planted in the Levante, can bring punchy acidity to a murky barrel of Monastrell, and some ***bodacious*** wineries are beginning to vinify it alone.

LANDMARK

The mind-bending moonscape of the Badlands of Gebas in the Sierra Espuña Regional Park is roughly equidistant from the towns of Bullas and Murcia, which share their names with the wine region and state, respectively.

DIGGING DEEPER

Valencia *(bah-LEN-see-ah)*/**Alicante** *(ah-lee-KAHN-teh)***:** Murcia's northern neighbor, the state of Valencia, is home to a wine region of the same name, along with the Alicante wine-growing zone. Both are ***valiant*** boosters of Monastrell, and critical attention is beginning to ***validate*** their commitment. The bold-fruited, big-bodied wines are ***alike*** those of Murcia.

Tempranillo *(TEM-prah-NEE-yoh)***:** Known locally as Cencibel *(SEN-see-BELL)*, this dignified northern grape—the star of Rioja and Ribera del Duero—is often blended with Monastrell in the Levante to lower its ***temperature***, so to speak.

WESTERN CAPE PINOTAGE

The barnacle-shaped chunk of land on South Africa's southwestern tip is known as the Western Cape. The northern half of that barnacle is the Coastal Region, which includes the city of Cape Town as well as Stellenbosch (STELL-en-BAHSH), arguably the epicenter of the South African fine wine industry.

SOUTH AFRICA

WESTERN CAPE

CAPE TOWN

TOP TERMS

Pinotage *(PEE-noh-tahj)*: A checkered winemaking past has created the *mirage*-like impression that this uniquely South African cross of **Pinot** Noir and Cinsault tastes terrible. Not true. Carefully crafted Pinotage can be powerful, smoky, and earthy, yet ethereal.

Stellenbosch: This Western Cape sub-zone surrounding the eponymous city of Stellenbosch was the birthplace of Pinotage. Hilly terrain, excellent soils, and breezes off False Bay make this a *stellar spot* for growing warm-weather grape varieties.

DIGGING DEEPER

Cabernet Sauvignon *(KAB-air-nay SOH-vin-YOHN)*/ **Merlot** *(MAIR-loh)*: These two are often *combined* with other red grapes or *married* to each other to make mocha-like, decadent reds.

Syrah *(sih-RAH)*/**Shiraz** *(shi-RAZZ)*: It goes by both names in South Africa, and shows real character when bottled alone, displaying notes of *cinnamon*,

CULTURAL SNAPSHOT

Influenced by Dutch, German, French, and Indonesian design, the Cape Dutch architectural style is as uniquely South African as Pinotage. Some of the most notable examples can be found on winery estates, such as Vergelegen.

Cape Fold Belt separates wine country from the Great Karoo Desert

cigar, licorice, seaweed, and *cinders*. It brings *cinnabar* color and depth to a blend.

LANDMARK

Intrepid hikers walking the Panorama Circuit in the Jonkershoek Nature Reserve can see why the Western Cape is such a terrific wine-growing region by climbing and taking in the views of the 4,000-foot (1,220-meter)-plus Guardian Peak. The Cape Fold Belt mountains separate the hot, arid Great Karoo Desert from the fertile maritime region.

GEO QUIZ

Paarl *(PAHRL)*: This region just north of Stellenbosch is in a valley that traps heat like a *parka*. So the reds of the two sub-zones are not exactly on *par*. Paarl's tend to be bigger and burlier, with higher alcohol.

Walker Bay: It would take all day and half the night to *walk* to Walker Bay from Stellenbosch. Here on the southern coast of the barnacle, the climate is surprisingly brisk, allowing for cool-climate grapes like Pinot Noir and Chardonnay to thrive.

BAROSSA VALLEY SHIRAZ

South Australia isn't the nation's southernmost state. It's merely south-central, bringing to mind Ice Cube's anthemic rap, "How to Survive in South-Central Los Angeles." Like the killa MCs of that era, the Syrahs of South Australia were big hits in the 1990s.

AUSTRALIA

BAROSSA
VALLEY

SOUTH AUSTRALIA   ADELAIDE

TOP TERMS

Barossa *(bah-RAH-sah or bah-ROH-sah)* **Valley**: The heart of the Australian wine industry is this tiny appellation about an hour's drive from the port city of Adelaide. The growing seasons tend to be hot here, making for big, ***brassy*** wines that can't be ignored. Think of a ***brass*** tuba, blasting out ***bass*** notes of powerful fruit. **Shiraz** *(shi-RAZZ)*: Where French Syrah (see p.136) can be somewhat surly, its twin, Aussie Shiraz, has ***razzmatazz***. In balmy South Australia, it puts on extra layers of blackberry jam and black pepper and accessorizes with toasty oak barrels. This wine displays so much ***razzle-dazzle*** that many wine lovers aren't aware that anything else is grown here.

OTHER OPTIONS

Cabernet Sauvignon *(KAB-air-nay SOH-vin-YOHN)*: Blending some racy, minty, chocolatey cab with burly, bold Shiraz is like taking a ***cab*** to an ever-so-slightly more ***suave*** party.

CULTURAL SNAPSHOT

Like Emperor Frederick "red Beard" ***Barbarossa***, the German king who had a habit of invading Italy, Barossa Valley Shiraz can be found in the **south**. It's also big, brawny, and red and has conquered the world.

The fertile, sun-soaked Barossa Valley is ideal for agriculture

LANDMARK

If there's a mascot for Aussie Shiraz, it's got to be the kangaroo. Most notably, the *red* kangaroo. And if there's one place you've gotta visit while in South Australia, it's Kangaroo Island. You can't miss it: It's the 2,738-square-km (1,701-square-mile) landmass that's bouncing with marsupials.

Kangaroo Island

EXTRA CREDIT

OUTSIDE BAROSSA VALLEY

Clare Valley: Eggplant-purple Shiraz might be the best-known wine of South Australia, but Clare Valley's claim to fame is a *clear* white wine, Riesling.

Coonawarra (KOON-ah-WAHR-ah): Consider the coat of the redbone *coonhound*: It's as ruddy as the soils of Coonawarra and as "soft" and "fleshy" as Coonawarra's red Cabernet Sauvignons.

Eden Valley: Like the *Garden of Eden*, the high-elevation vineyards of Barossa Valley's next-door neighbor are as old as, well, 1847, anyway, and biblically bounteous, bearing fruits of Shiraz, Riesling, Cabernet Sauvignon, Viognier, and more.

McLaren Vale: The Shiraz from this milder Mediterranean climate might be slightly less blustery than that of the Barossa Valley, but it can still be as knock-you-down strong as a *maritime gale*.

MARGARET RIVER CABERNET

Western Australia: In the American West, *folks like to eat* southwestern-*style food. If Western Australia is a* quesadilla, *its wine country is a teeny-tiny bite out of the lower left-hand corner. And Cabernet is surprisingly tasty with* quesadillas.

AUSTRALIA

WESTERN AUSTRALIA
MARGARET RIVER

TOP TERMS

Cabernet Sauvignon *(KAB-air-nay SOH-vin-YOHN)*: Life is a "*cabaret*" on Australia's gorgeous wine-soaked west coast. And cabaret is a fittingly French word because Margaret River wine is considered to be the most French, stylistically speaking, of Australia.

Margaret River: *Margaret Thatcher* and Margaret River wines might both be described as "elegant," but that's where the similarity ends. While Mrs Thatcher leaned to the right, Margaret River is a surfer's paradise, hanging ten on the wayyy left coast of Australia.

OTHER OPTIONS

Merlot *(MAIR-loh)*: It's increasingly popular here to blend *mellow* Merlot with Cabernet Sauvignon to make a *Bordeaux*-style wine. Merlot brings a *marshmallow*-like softness and sweetness to gravelly Cab.

Shiraz *(shi-RAZZ)*: In the cooler coastal zones, this region makes a more elegant, *sheer* style of Shiraz, with brambly notes.

CULTURAL SNAPSHOT

What is *Baroness Margaret Thatcher* thinking about in this photo? Eucalyptus. It's the favorite food of cuddly koalas. It thrives in Margaret River's Mediterranean climate, and it's an aromatic component in Cabernet Sauvignon.

LANDMARK

Western Australia's southwestern-most point is Cape Leeuwin, situated in a stunning seaside national park. Its defining landmark is a lighthouse, planted on a spit that juts out to mark the point where the Indian Ocean meets the Southern Ocean. Wine enthusiasts often describe the region's climate as "Mediterranean," but if you envision that lighthouse, buffeted by squalls, you'll get a sense of the strength and character that Margaret River's grapes are noted for.

The lighthouse at Cape Leeuwin

FOR CONTRARIANS

Chardonnay *(SHAHR-doh-nay)*: What rhymes with Cabernet and cabaret? *Rays* of sunny Chardonnay. Margaret River Chard at its best gets zip and acidity from those coastal breezes and a pleasing plumpness from that beach-babe sunshine.

Semillon/Sauvignon Blanc *(seh-mee-YOH/SOH-vin-YOH blahnk)*: A strong and citrusy Bordeaux-style white blend that's best enjoyed young—when, like a perky kid on a *see-saw*, it's got spunk.

Early morning mists in Margaret River

EXTRA CREDIT

OUTSIDE MARGARET RIVER

Great Southern: This one's a snap—it's the biggest (*greatest*) and most *southerly* wine region of Western Australia.

Frankland River: Hidden high in rolling hills inside Great Southern, breezy Frankland River is nearly free of pests and diseases, and thus, like Doctor ***Frankenstein***, can turn just about any assemblage of body parts— I mean grapevines—into a living, breathing … wine. However, while it's a jumble of Cabernet Sauvignon, Riesling, Shiraz, Viognier, Chardonnay, Sauvignon Blanc, Merlot, Malbec, and more, there's nothing monstrous about it.

NIAGARA PENINSULA ICEWINE

Ontario, in eastern Canada, is shaped like a fat fish that swims between Hudson Bay at the north and the Great Lakes to its south. Ontario's wine regions can all be found in the fish's tail fin.

CANADA

ONTARIO

NIAGARA PENINSULA

TOP TERMS

Icewine: A style of sweet *wine* made from *ice*-cold frozen fruit, most commonly Riesling and Vidal. It can also be produced from red grapes like Cabernet Franc.

Niagara Peninsula: It's the only wine region in the world with enough reliable freezing days to turn out Icewine year after year. How cold does it get here? Not only do those massive lakes ice over, but sometimes even the fast-moving *Niagara Falls* freeze to a halt.

KEY PLAYERS

Riesling *(REEZ-ling)*: In some quarters, it can be slightly insulting to use the S-word in regards to Riesling (it's "fruity," not "sweet," okay?). But when frozen and vinified on the Niagara Peninsula, this grape is *reaching* its peak of sweetness and saturation.

Vidal *(vee-DAAL)*: An otherwise-unremarkable hybrid grape, Vidal isn't *vital* to wine lovers or winemakers unless Icewine is on the agenda. In which case it makes a treat so marmaladey that it might perk up a person's *vital* signs.

CULTURAL SNAPSHOT

You know those daredevils who ride over Niagara Falls in a barrel? Icewine producers are nearly as foolhardy, hand-picking each frozen-solid grape in temperatures lower than -8°C (17°F) and conducting their winemaking in sub-freezing conditions.

Who needs to see Niagara Falls when there are wineries nearby?

LANDMARK

Buffalo, New York, is just across the border from Niagara wine country, a drive of approximately thirty minutes. When you're downtown, don't miss Fountain Plaza, where you can ice skate at Rotary Rink for free. It's frozen. Just like the grapes are.

OTHER OPTIONS

Chardonnay *(SHAHR-doh-NAY)*: You cannot drink sweet wine all day. Fortunately, it's *in the cards* for Ontario to be a great Chardonnay producer. Smooth and vibrant, Ontario Chards lean toward crisp acidity and sweet citrus notes.

Pinot Noir *(PEE-noh NWAHR)*: The deck is stacked for breezy, water-bound Ontario to make great cool-climate Pinot Noir. The grapes, like the ten of clubs, are plentiful and black. The acidity is diamond-sharp. The red-berry-and-bramble flavors are like hearts and spades.

EXTRA CREDIT

WARMER WINEMAKING IN THE WEST

Ontario's eastern seaboard and lakefront wine regions might be better-known, but all the way over on the west coast of Canada, just north of Washington State, British Columbia is equally strong and arguably more diverse.

In the Okanagan (**OHK-uh-NAH-gun**) Valley, the vineyards overlooking picturesque Lake Okanagan are warm enough to support oak-worthy varietals like Syrah, Merlot, and Cabernet Sauvignon, while in cooler parts, like Kelowna (**keh-LAU-nah**), Pinot Noir and Chardonnay rule. There is even an exciting growing movement in sparkling wine production. Get that into your *noggin*.

LOIRE CHENIN BLANC

LOIRE

FRANCE

What's the best thing about biting into a cream puff, jelly donut, or pain au chocolat? The sweetest part is hidden in the middle. And what's sweetest about the lengthy Loire is the center section, where Anjou, Saumur, and Touraine specialize in delicious dessert wines.

TOP TERMS

Anjou *(AH-zhoo)*: The Loire region of Anjou is known for producing a variety of wine styles and colors, but if *angels* and *ingenues* were to agree to drink just one, it would have to be heaven-sent sweet Chenin Blanc.

Chenin Blanc *(SHUH-nuh BLAH)*: Just about anywhere in the Loire where Chenin Blanc is grown, a wide variety of wines can be made out of it, including dry and crisp; sparkling; and rich and unctuous. Then there's the sweet form. It's as though a *shaman* has burned a spicy incense over a bottle of *white* fungus-covered raisins (see Noble Rot, right) and created liquid gold.

GEO QUIZ

Coteaux du Layon *(KOHT-oh doo LAY-oh)*: At the end of a long dinner, when you're longing for a *cot to lay on*, perk yourself up with a decadent sweet wine from this northwestern part of Anjou. It's humid enough here every fall to get Chenin Blanc grapes super-ripe and even deliciously rotten.

CULTURAL SNAPSHOT

If you're visiting the region, be sure to try Crémet d'Anjou, a whipped *fromage blanc* confection that's typically served with fresh local d'Anjou pears. It's like the edible version of Loire's sweet wines—silky-smooth, unctuous yet weightless.

Dessert for the eyes: Château d'Azay-le-Rideau

Quarts de Chaume *(KAH duh SHOHM)*: The best-known sweet wine appellation within the Coteaux du Layon. Quarts and *quarts of charming* dessert-style Chenin are produced here.

LANDMARK

The Loire is famous for its fairytale castles. The sixteenth-century white Château d'Azay-le-Rideau is as closely connected to the waters of the Loire as the white grapes that grow all along the river's banks. Sturdily built for longevity, with delicate details and spiky turrets, it's as age-worthy, elegant, and fine-pointed as a Loire sweet white wine.

DIGGING DEEPER

Botrytis cinerea *(boh-TRY-tis sin-AIR-ee-yah)*: As any *botanist* will tell you, ripe grapes growing in the *area* of a humid confluence of a number of rivers and streams (ahem, Coteaux du Layon) have a tendency to *sin*, growing this gray fruit fungus, aka **Noble Rot**. The affected white Chenin grapes shrivel into sinfully sweet yellow raisins, which make a wine gold in color, spicy and rich, with baked-pear flavors and fresh acidity.

BORDEAUX SAUTERNES SÉMILLON

The Gironde estuary is an arrow pointing straight at Bordeaux's sweet wine sector. Sauternes and Barsac are located on the lower Left Bank, inside the Graves region, approximately 35 miles (56 km) southeast of the city of Bordeaux.

FRANCE

BORDEAUX

TOP TERMS

Barsac *(BAR-suck)*: Barsac is not *far* from the village of Sauternes, and Barsac wineries can *barter* for whichever of the two appellation names they wish to print on their labels. (Insiders contend that Barsac is the secret *star* of the region.) A bit lighter and fresher than its peer, Barsac makes a sweet match with a cheese course.

Sauternes *(SOH-tairn)*: Gold in its youth, turning amber with age, Sauternes wine looks like it has been *sautéed* in butter. It's also located in *southeast* Bordeaux.

KEY PLAYERS

Sémillon *(seh-mee-YOH)*: Sauternes tends to be sold in *semi*, or half-sized, bottles. The key grape of Sauternes and Barsac is Sémillon, which takes on a waxy, ripe-apricot character when it's got Noble Rot.

Sauvignon Blanc *(SOH-vee-YOH BLAH)*: When you have an infection, a nurse garbed in pristine *white* cures you. When this white grape has an infection, it gets squashed and squeezed by a winemaker garbed in grubbies.

CULTURAL SNAPSHOT

It is said that the most alluring aromas contain a hint of something vile. Gastronomes drool over foie gras, which, frankly, smells of carrion. Sauternes, another disturbingly delicious delicacy, is mind-blowingly good with ... foie gras.

Château Malromé's yellow walls—as butter-yellow as a glass of Sauternes

LANDMARK

The palace walls at Château Malromé are as butter-yellow as a glass of Sauternes. The grounds include a winery and one-hundred-acre vineyard; a guided tour finishes with a tasting. But the real draw is the château's most famous resident. Henri de Toulouse-Lautrec was an immensely talented painter who, tragically, suffered from a bone disease that caused him to die before his thirty-seventh birthday. Like a Sémillon grape afflicted with Noble Rot, the artist flourished intellectually and creatively even while his body wasted away.

DIGGING DEEPER

Botrytis cinerea (boh-TRY-tis sin-AIR-ee-yah): *Righteous* nineteenth-century missionaries who stayed too long in Africa eventually came down with **malaria**. Leave ripe grapes on the vine in foggy Sauternes and they grow this gray fruit fungus, *Botrytis cinerea.*

Noble Rot: Or *Botrytis cinerea.* Good news is, rather than rotting the fruit, botrytis nobly shrivels Sémillon and Sauv Blanc grapes into sinfully sweet (if unattractive) raisins. Those missionaries saw their duty as **noble**, but many natives thought they were preaching a bunch of **rot**.

EXTRA CREDIT

FRANCE'S FORTIFIED DESSERT WINES

....

When you're perusing the sweet section of a restaurant menu, you might see the following wines listed along with Sauternes and Barsac. They're sweet not from Noble Rot but from being fortified with brandy before all the sugar has fermented into alcohol.

....

Banyuls (BAN-yools): Balmy Banyuls soaks up the sun from its home on the Spanish border and the Mediterranean Sea. Here, (mostly) red grapes are vinifed, fortified with brandy, aged in oak barrels, and left out in the heat to cook. The result is a wine that's as sun-baked **brown** as the Diet Cokes being consumed on the Banyuls beach.

....

Muscat de ... (moos-KHAT duh ...): Whether it's from the Southern Rhône River Valley (Muscat de Beaumes-de-Venise), the Languedoc (Muscat de Frontignan), or Roussillon (Muscat de Rivesaltes), just know this: These are all fortified sweet wines made from the **musky** Muscat grape. They're as yellow as honey and smell deliciously of roasted pineapple and ultra-ripe **muskmelon**.

COGNAC UGNI BLANC

Bordeaux's northern neighbor on the central-west coast of France isn't famous for wine, but wine-based spirits. Organized like an oblong target over the Charente River, Cognac (COH-nyac) *quality improves as you move inward along (more or less) concentric rings, with the best vineyards located around the bull's eye of the town of Segonzac.*

FRANCE

COGNAC

TOP TERM

Cognac: A celebrated 40%ABV brandy distilled from wine grapes and aged in barrels. Like a designer leather *cognac-colored handbag*, Cognac is a smooth, amber-hued status symbol.

OTHER OPTIONS

Armagnac *(AHR-mah-nyac)*: This brandy is made in the Gascony region, about 100 miles (161 km) to the south. It's considered more historic and *artisanal* than corporate Cognac.

Calvados *(CAL-vah-dohss)*: A fine apple (not grape!) brandy, produced on the north coast of France from dry cider. It might have the color and aroma of *caramel* but don't consume it with abandon, just a small *dose* will do.

Pineau des Charentes *(PEE-noh day SHAH-rahnt)*: A *charlatan* wine, usually white, but also rosé and red, from the Cognac region. Its *penal* offense? Inebriation: It's fortified with Cognac. Serve it as an apéritif, over ice, with an orange wedge.

CULTURAL SNAPSHOT

The Limousin region, famous for its oak barrels, overlaps Cognac. Due to the wood's wide grain and porosity, these casks are perfect for aging Cognac and other fine spirits. Enjoy the coincidence, if you happen to sip Cognac in a *limousine*.

LANDMARK

The Cognac region got into distilling because its climate is too damp for quality winemaking. Here's proof: Marais Poitevin, in Cognac country, was once a swamp. Fifteenth-century monks drained it, creating a marshland broken up into islands and canals. Tourists visiting this Venise Verte, or "Green Venice," take riverboat tours and rent rowboats to navigate the brackish waters.

MORE TERMS TO KNOW

XO: *Extra-old* Cognac is considered the best because it has aged the longest, to build the most complex, nutty, fruity, and honeyed aromas. If someone gives you a bottle, give them a ***hug and a kiss***.

VSOP: *Very special old pale* Cognac has aged at least four years in large barrels, called casks. You'd be ***very sopping*** if you were in a barrel of Cognac for that long.

VS: A *very special*—but not extraordinarily special— Cognac that has aged at least two years in casks. It's like a gift of satin pajamas from ***Victoria's Secret***: Nice, but not exactly La Perla.

Marais Poitevin, the "Green Venice" of France

RHEINGAU RIESLING

Combine the Rheingau (RINE-gow) *with Nahe* (NAH-eh)*, Rheinhessen* (RINE-hess-un)*, and Pfalz* (FAALZ) *on a map and you'll see a candy-cane shape. Like their better-known neighbor, the Mosel, they all produce dessert wines that will satisfy your sweet tooth without cloying like candy. They all make fine dry Rieslings, as well.*

GERMANY
NAHE
RHEINGAU
RHEINHESSEN
PFALZ

TOP TERMS

Riesling *(REEZ-ling)*: Left on the vine late into the season, Riesling loses all **reason** and develops Noble Rot (or *Botrytis cinerea*), a gray fungus, and the fruit is **reborn** as flavorful raisins.

Beerenauslese *(BARE-un-OWS-lay-zuh)*: Appropriate for serving to a **bear now or later**, because it's made from raisins and is as golden and sweet as honey.

DIGGING DEEPER

Trockenbeerenauslese *(TRAHK-un-BARE-un-OWS-lay-zuh)*: Even sweeter than a Beerenauslese, made from even-more-shriveled raisins. Extremely rare and quite pricey, its apricot-jam flavors could attract a **truckload** of **bears**.

Eiswein *(ICE-vine)*: **Ice balls** (actually, they're frozen grapes) harvested during freezing-cold weather and pressed in a chilly winery render nectar-sweet juice that makes an **Icewine** that even the Snow Queen would love.

CULTURAL SNAPSHOT

Idar-Oberstein in Nahr is Germany's gem-cutting capital due to its rich agate deposits. Agate is a gorgeous waxy stone growing in volcanic rocks. Noble Rot is a fungus growing in grapes, making gorgeous, waxy wine.

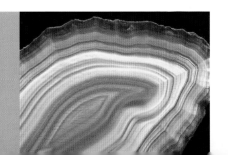

LANDMARK

In the Rheinhessen, at Worms, the Nibelungen Bridge crosses the great Rhine River. It's named for the ancient Nibelung myths, which became a twelfth-century epic poem and the basis for Wagner's *Der Ring des Nibelungen (The Ring Cycle)* of four operas. In these stories, a ridiculous amount of pique over social rank results in all sorts of murder, sex, and dragon-slaying. Likewise, the damp mist off the river makes chaos in the vineyards. And outsiders find the complex classifications and rankings of German Rieslings to be a bit over-the-top. But then you taste one of these wines … and you hear music.

GEO QUIZ

Nahe: On a map of our four German regions, Nahe forms the curled tip of the candy cane. It's noted for its elegant Rieslings that are *nigh (nearly)* identical to the Mosel's.

Pfalz: Forming the shaft of the candy cane, the Pfalz is a *faultlessly* multi-talented growing region, as adept at dry table wines (such as Spatburgunder, aka Pinot Noir) as dessert wines.

Rheinhessen: Located at the base of the candy cane's curve, Rheinhessen produces the highest volume of quality wine in Germany. Since it's on the *Rhine,* it doesn't take much *guessing* to conclude that this area also makes sweet wines.

The Nibelungen Bridge on the Rhine River—can you hear Wagner?

EXTRA CREDIT
SEKT

In Germany and Austria, most sparkling wine is called "Sekt," and it's often made from Riesling grapes. There are two **sects**: There is a clean, simple style made by the same method as Prosecco—that is, in a sealed steel tank. Then there is a richer, more expensive style that's fermented in the bottle, as Champagne is. As if you weren't already confused enough by all the Riesling terminology, the word **Trocken**, which means "dry" on a still wine label, means "off dry" on a Sekt label; so you might see it in the sweet **section** of the wine list. Dry Sekt is labeled "brut." The name "Sekt" is also liable to trip you up. Because if you've been studying wine a bit, you might know by now that "*sec*," "*secco*," and "*seco*" mean "dry" in French, Italian, and Spanish. Don't even try to *dissect* this quagmire; just drink that glass of Sekt.

TOKAJ TOKAJI ASZÚ

Just south of the Slovakian border and a stone's throw from Ukraine, the Tokaj (TOHK-eye) wine region looks like a miniature duplicate of the nation of Hungary. Both are shaped like magic lamps, with the fairy-tale land of Tokaj occupying Hungary's northeastern spout.

TOKAJ

HUNGARY

TOP TERMS

Tokaji Aszú *(toh-KAH-yee ah-SZHOO)*: Hungary's world-famous dessert drink gets its name from its home (the Tokaj region) plus Aszú, a ***toffee***-like paste that's ***added to*** dry white wine.

Furmint *(FOOR-meent)*: The top grape in Tokaj is first ***fermented*** into a dry white wine. It can be bottled on its own or made into a sweet wine with a second ***fermentation***.

MORE TERMS TO KNOW

Aszú *(ah-SZHOO)*: During harvest, winemakers carefully sort out grapes that have been shriveled into raisins by Noble Rot, aka *Botrytis cinerea*. They smash this super-sweet fruit to make Aszú paste, then ***add it to*** dry Furmint wine to make sweet Tokaji Aszú.

Puttonyos *(POO-toh-NYOHS)*: A number ranging from 3 to 6 Puttonyos indicates the amount of Aszú ***put into*** the wine and thus translates into the sugar level of the resulting Tokaji Aszú. If you're going to be drinking a

CULTURAL SNAPSHOT

With its pinprick acidity, copper color, and silky texture, a fine glass of Tokaji Aszú shares traits with (stay with me here) Hungary's national dog breed, the Viszla: A russet-coated canine, sleek and smooth, with a sharp nose and elegant point.

Tokaj, world famous for its Tokaji wine

6 Puttonyos Tokaji tonight, you'd better **put on your** running shoes now.

LANDMARK

The elegant white egret, beloved by northeastern Hungarians, is an indicator that the Tokaj region is the ideal place to make dessert wine. Where the Bodrog and Tisza Rivers meet, a mist engulfs the grapevines of Tokaj, inducing Noble Rot to set in. And a nearby wetland, the Tokaj-Bodrogzug Protected Landscape Area, floods every spring, creating a playground for water birds.

DIGGING DEEPER

Aszú Eszencia *(ah-ZHOO ESS-ent-ZEE-ah)*: When Aszú grapes are pressed, the first juice to spill out is like the **essence** of honey. It takes years to ferment into a wine-like **ambrosia** that is nearly all sugar, has barely any alcohol, and can age for eons in your cellar.

Hárslevelű *(HAHR-shleh-VELL-oo)*: It may be **harsh** of me to ask, but try to **say** this grape's name, or **spell it—can you**? The secondary grape of Tokaj is often blended with Furmint and sometimes bottled on its own, as a dry or sweet wine. Like Sauvignon Blanc in Bordeaux, dry Hárslevelű is maybe a little bit **harsh** and herbaceous, but as a dessert wine, it's smooth as **velour**.

EXTRA CREDIT

HUNGARIAN REDS

If you're **hungry** for a hearty Hungarian red wine, don't despair. Despite the fame of its sweet and dry white wines, Hungary also produces outstanding savory reds. The hot region for them—in more ways than one—is balmy Villány, near the Croatian border. Its volcanic soils are well-suited to Bordeaux varieties like Cabernet Sauvignon and Merlot, but critics think Cabernet Franc might hold the most promise. Of the many indigenous grapes, **Kékfrankos (kek-FRANK-osh)** is the most prominent. It's identical to the Austrian Blaufränkish and makes delicious spicy wines, bright ruby in color, with notes of sour red cherries. And the most famous of all Hungarian reds is a blend of nine grapes called Bull's Blood. It's called **Bikavér (BEEK-ah-VEE-yur)** in Hungarian, and it's as dark as, well, **Bull's Blood**.

VENETO GRAPPA

Grappa (GRAH-pah) *can be made from any wine grape, in any Italian wine region. But the Veneto* (VEH-neh-toh) *and Friuli* (free-OO-lee), *which surround Venice like a bunch of grapes, are home to the nation's best distillers. Veneto is the most productive, while the modern artisanal movement to distill single-variety grappas from high-quality wine grapes started in Friuli.*

FRIULI-VENEZIA GIULIA
VENETO
ITALY

TOP TERMS

Grappa: After *grapes* are crushed, the pips (seeds), stems, and skins left in the wine press are called "pomace." Grappa is made by distilling pomace into wine grape brandy.
Picolit *(PEE-koh-LEET)*: In the Veneto, Amarone, Prosecco, and Moscato are commonly used to make grappa. In Friuli, the rare and *peevish* Picolit makes ambrosial dessert wines and a brandy that will make you so giddy, you'll be playing *peek-a-boo.*

GEO QUIZ

Südtiroler *(SOOD-tee-ROH-ler)* **Grappa/ Grappa dell'Alto Adige** *(dell-AHL-toh AH-dee-jay)*/ **Grappa del Trentino** *(dell tren-TEE-noh)*: It sounds like *sooty roller*, but it's the German term for "South Tyrol," aka Trentino-Alto Adige. The variety of grapes used here ranges from *high-altitude* Gewürztraminer to *trendy Teroldego.*
Grappa del Piemonte *(dell pee-ay-MOHN-tay)*: The Nebbiolo zones of Barolo and Barbaresco are identified

CULTURAL SNAPSHOT

Grappa was once barely potable firewater. Today's silky artisanal grappas are handcrafted in copper stills. Chill young grappas and serve them in narrow, tulip-shaped glasses. Wider Cognac snifters are better for savoring barrel-aged styles.

Bassano del Grappa's Ponte Vecchio was designed by Andrea Palladio

by name on grappa labels. The tradition in **Piedmont** is to go the *full monte* and distill fermented rather than raw pomace, from Moscato and Nebbiolo grapes.

Grappa della Toscana *(dell-ah toh-SKAH-nah)*: *Tuscan* wine estates might sell grappa made from their own wine grapes, but *tell your mamma* that these are typically distilled outside the region and trucked back to the winery to be sold.

Grappa di Sicilia *(dee see-CHEEL-yah)*: Across the *sea* of *teal*, the southern island of **Sicily** has a buzzing grappa market, variable in quality, starring the red Nero d'Avola grape and dessert-wine bases such as Moscato di Pantelleria and Marsala.

LANDMARK

Some say that the name of Monte Grappa comes from a dialect term for "crag," while the drink's title comes from *grappolo*, for a cluster of grapes. Others claim the mountain, and the town at its base, were the birthplace of grappa. At any rate, the Poli Museo della Grappa is well worth a visit. It's located on the east side of Bassano del Grappa's landmark Ponte Vecchio, a sixteenth-century wooden pontoon bridge designed by famed architect Andrea Palladio.

TUSCAN VIN SANTO

Tuscany, or Toscana *(toh-SKAH-nah)*
in Italian, is sliced out of central-western
Italy like an oversized piece of cake—and
cake (from whichever mamma is doing the
baking) is delicious paired with a glass of
Vin Santo from this region. That said, the
arduous process of producing Vin Santo
isn't exactly a piece of cake.

TUSCANY

ITALY

TOP TERMS

Passito *(pah-SEE-toh)*: After harvest, the winemaker *bypasses* the usual step of crushing the ripe grapes, instead laying them out to dry (sometimes on straw mats) and shrivel into sweet raisins.

Vin Santo *(vin SAHN-toh)*: Pressed raisins make a sweet, syrupy wine that traditionally was used in the celebration of the Eucharist during mass—hence, it's the "*saint's wine.*" Aging in barrels with plenty of air space oxidizes the liquid, giving it a caramel color and nutty aroma.

DIGGING DEEPER

Occhio di Pernice *(OH-kee-yoh dee pair-NEE-chay)*: This rare, molasses-like Vin Santo made from red Sangiovese grapes ranges in color from pink to garnet to *ochre* and doesn't fit in any *food-pairing niche* …. Try it with anything from salty cheese to dried fruit.

Recioto della Valpolicella *(reh-CHOH-toh dell-ah VAHL-pohl-ee-CHELL-ah)*: A red passito wine, made in northeastern Italy's Valpolicella region, which tastes like

CULTURAL SNAPSHOT

Originally invented to withstand Roman military campaigns, biscotti are today a specialty of Tuscany. These almond biscuits, called *cantucci* or *cantuccini* in these parts, are ideal for dunking into a glass of Vin Santo.

Vin Santo grapes drying on racks

sweet black cherry juice. Here's a ***recipe*** for a delicious romantic evening: A ***delectable*** glass of Recioto and ***pole-dancing*** to the strains of ***cello*** music. As one does.

LANDMARK

It turns out that passito-style Vin Santo wines aren't the only delicious beneficiaries of Tuscany's relentless sunshine, dry heat, and strong breezes. Wine critics frequently use "dried figs" to describe the flavor of Vin Santo. Which is fitting, because Tuscany—and the town of Carmignano in particular—is renowned for its dried figs. Other famous sun-dried Tuscan products include salty shriveled olives and savory sun-dried tomatoes.

DON'T STOP

Picolit (*PEE-koh-LEET*): Italy's rare and coveted answer to France's Sauternes is worth getting to know. It comes from Friuli, in northeastern Italy, and is made from low-yielding Picolit grapes. The fruit is either dried *à la passito*, or simply left to hang on the vine late into the harvest season, where the delicate, *piccolo* (tiny) grapes shrivel into delicious raisins.

Vino Liquoroso (*VEE-noh LIK-ohr-OH-zoh*): Any Italian wine that has been fortified by the addition of ***liquor***. Vin Santo Liquoroso is just one of many styles; it's made all over Italy, from a variety of grapes.

DOURO PORT

The commercial center of the Port wine trade is the city of Oporto on the Atlantic Coast, but the grapes are grown closer to the valley's eastern border with Spain. The Douro (DOH-roh) River Valley cuts through the top of Portugal like the furrow that scores the upper squares of a dark chocolate bar. Which is one of the many foods that's delicious paired with Port.

DOURO
OPORTO
PORTUGAL

TOP TERMS

Porto *(POHR-toh)*/**Port**: Although the grapes are grown along the Douro Valley, barrel-aging happens in the *port* city of Oporto, where the wine is blended and bottled. Labels are printed with either the shortened "Porto," or the Anglicized "Port."

Ruby Port: The most basic Port style is made from a blend of many different red grapes—too many to list here. The winemaking process aims to extract as much *ruby* color and cherry flavor as possible before fermentation is stopped dead in its tracks by the addition of brandy, making a fortified wine.

DIGGING DEEPER

Reserve: The best of the basic Rubies are *reserved* for these special blends, which sometimes are labeled with the tautological term "Special" in addition to "Reserve." These popular bottlings often bear special names and tend to be priced reasonably.

Late-Bottled Vintage: Also labeled "LBV," these are

The Douro's terraced slopes look as if they were carved with a chisel

Rubies from a single **vintage** that have been **bottled later,** after four to six years of cellar age in giant wooden vats.
Vintage: In only the very best **vintage** years, the very finest wines are set aside to age two years in casks, then an additional decade or more in bottle prior to release. Vintage Ports are rare and can be quite pricey.

LANDMARK

High in the hills overlooking the Douro River, the sanctuary of São Salvador do Mundo is an excellent vantage point for surveying the whole valley. Over thousands of years, viticulture has shaped the landscape into step-like terraces.

DON'T STOP THERE

Tawny: Oak-barrel aging and oxygen exposure turns these Ports a **tawny** color over time. Higher-quality Tawnies are labeled 10-Year-Old, 20-Year-Old, and so on. These numbers don't represent the actual age of the wine, but the average age of the wines, from a number of barrels, which have been blended together.
Colheita *(KOH-lay-tah)*: Better barrels of Tawny Port, set aside to age on their own for a minimum of seven years until they are a warm **cola color,** are bottled as Colheitas. These aren't meant for aging; they're considered to be somewhat better than a 10-Year-Old Tawny.

MADEIRA MALMSEY

In centuries past, ships crossing the Atlantic stopped at the island of Madeira (mah-DAY-rah) to load up on sugarcane and fortified wine. When they set sail again, these ships' hulls were cooked by tropical temperatures and agitated by rocking waves. Below decks, the barrels of fortified wine transformed into one-of-a-kind Madeira.

PORTUGAL

MADEIRA

TOP TERMS

Madeira: A fortified wine that's exposed to oxygen and heat but *magically* isn't ruined, Madeira is tawny to *mahogany* in color, while on the palate it's sweet, fruity, acidic, salty, and bitter all at once.

Malmsey *(MAHLM-zee)*: Also known as Malvasia *(MAHL-vah-ZEE-ah)*, the Malmsey grape makes the richest style of Madeira. It looks like coffee, feels like molasses, and tastes sweet like toffee yet tangy like *malt whiskey*. It's magnificent with warm gingerbread.

DIGGING DEEPER

5-, 10-, 15-, 20-Year-Old: Like many Sherries and some Ports, these Madeiras are made by mixing older barrels to arrive at an average age.

Reserve/Special/Extra: These *extra* words on a label refer to the period of time the wine was aged prior to release, whether it was *reserved* for five years; is *special* because it's at least ten; or had an *extra-long* wait of at least twenty years.

CULTURAL SNAPSHOT

Madeira may look like a beachy paradise, but its best vineyards grow on precipitous mountainsides. To get a feel for the incline, slide down Funchal's streets in a wood-wicker toboggan. Recover with a soothing glass of Madeira.

Colheita *(KOH-lay-tah)*: A young **colt** of a vintage Madeira, it ages in casks (large barrels) between five and eighteen years prior to bottling and release. The labels sometimes say "Harvest" rather than "Colheita."

Vintage/Frasqueira *(frah-SKAIR-uh)*: The most prized and pricey Madeiras, aged in casks for a minimum of twenty years prior to release. A detail **Franz Kafka** would appreciate, these **vintage-dated** wines can cellar-age for more than two centuries and still taste superb.

LANDMARK

The slopes of Madeira are sliced up by thousands of miniature canals. First developed in the sixteenth century, these historic *levadas* transport water for hydroelectric power and irrigation of crops, including grapevines. You can hike along many of them, but some are perilous, with drops and tunnel sections, so choose your path carefully.

DIGGING DEEPER

Bual *(BOO-ahl)*: Slightly lighter and more savory than Malmsey, its aromatics are like the toppings for a **bowl** of oatmeal: maple syrup, brown sugar, and cinnamon.

Verdelho *(vehr-DELL-oh)*: Like a **bordello** in the Wild West, copper-colored Verdelho is sweet and salty, tart, and leathery. It's drier and lighter than Bual.

Sercial *(SAIR-see-ahl)*: Amber-colored Sercial, the **sparest of the series**, is citrusy and **sherry-like**, with nutty notes and plenty of acidity. Try it as an apéritif, or serve with light seafood dishes.

Watch your step as you hike alongside a levada

Heat, oxygen, and casks contribute to the mystery that is Madeira

EXTRA CREDIT

3-YEAR-OLDS AND RAIN

Official category: Perhaps our subconscious associations with fitful toddlers explains why "3-Year-Old," an official Madeira category, is almost never printed on labels. However, these wines can be affordable delights for everyday drinking and tend to go by special proprietary names, such as "Blandy's Duke of Cumberland."

Rainwater: Back in the days before steamships and refrigerated containers, Madeira made it across the Atlantic unscathed and became a favorite tipple of Revolutionary-era Americans. A very pale, off-dry style called "Rainwater" was preferred by the Yankee populace, but it never caught on in other parts of the world. Rainwater is still sold in the US market; quality runs the gamut.

JEREZ SHERRY

Down in Andalucia (AHN-dah-loo-SEE-ah), where the southern tip of Spain puckers up across the Strait of Gibraltar to give Morocco a kiss, the "Sherry Triangle" of vineyards surrounds the towns of Jerez de la Frontera, El Puerto de Santa Maria, and Sanlúcar de Barrameda.

SPAIN

JEREZ

ANDALUCIA

TOP TERMS

Fino *(FEE-noh)*: Like a *feeble* cobweb of sea foam, Fino is a diaphanous, tangy, salty apéritif-style Sherry made from the Palomino *(PAH-loh-MEE-noh)* grape. Its funky flavor comes from a yeast called *flor* that's more like a ceiling than a *floor*: It blankets the tops of the barrels, so that the wine *sees no* oxygen.

Manzanilla *(MAHN-zah-NEE-yah)*: Manzanilla is *managed* the same way as Fino in the winery, but it's from *Tanzania.* Just kidding. It's actually from a specific sub-zone around the town of Sanlúcar de Barrameda.

DIGGING DEEPER

Amontillado *(ah-MOHN-tee-YAH-doh)*/**Palo Cortado** *(PAH-loh kor-TAH-doh)*: Fino aged in barrels for fifteen years eventually goes *incommunicado* when it loses its protective flor. Exposed to oxygen, it becomes amber-colored, nutty, savory Amontillado. *Aficionados* love its sibling Palo Cortado, which loses its flor and its *pallor* early, turning a deep molasses color.

Oloroso *(OH-loh-ROH-soh)*: The big brown *oso* (bear) of Sherries gets a quick, *furioso* fortification right off the bat, killing the flor and retaining a touch of sweetness. Allowed to age with plenty of breathing room, Oloroso takes on a cola color and notes of toasted nuts.

Pedro Ximénez *(PEH-droh hee-MEH-neth)* **or PX:** *Peter Hemingway* is a Spanish grape that's laid out in the sun to raisin before being made into a fortified wine.

LANDMARK

The white albariza soil of the Jerez region hogs the credit for creating the ideal environment for Sherry grapes. But as any kiteboarder will tell you, there are two natural advantages to the southern coast of Spain. Sherry vineyards benefit from the *levante*, a dry warm gust from the east that ripens grapes. And wineries are built open-ended to take advantage of the *poniente*, a wet, cool breeze from the ocean that gives the wines their briny flavor and aids in the growth of flor yeasts.

DON'T STOP

En Rama *(en RAH-mah)*: Translated as "*raw*," this term is printed on *rare* unfiltered Sherries. No, they don't quite look like snow-globe *dioramas*, but these cult favorites do tend to have a few harmless yeast chunks floating around in them.

JEREZ
XERES
SHERRY
MANZANILLA

DENOMINACIONES
■ DE ORIGEN ■

"Sherry" in English, Spanish, French

SO WHAT'S A SOLERA?

Most Sherries are not vintage-dated. Instead, they are classified by their average age. In a **solera** *(soh-LEH-ah)* system, large barrels are stacked atop one another with the oldest wines occupying the bottom row and the current vintage on top. Every year, the winemaker removes wine from each barrel to blend and then fills the empty space with more recent vintages.

VOS/VORS: These letters are a Latin abbreviation, but most people refer to them as **Very Old Sherry** or **Very Old Rare Sherry**. VOS are at least twenty years old, and VORS are at least thirty.

Añada *(ahn-YAH-dah)*: Labels printed with a year (that's an *año* en *Español*) and the word "añada" are found on extremely rare vintage-dated Sherries.

Sherry's secret sauce: ocean breezes from two directions

Chapter Four

REVERSE THE POWER STRUCTURE

How do you fake your way through a wine list? By adopting the right attitude. In this chapter, we'll learn how to turn the table on uncomfortable wine moments, read through the lines of confusing menus, and take charge of a group of dining companions when you'd rather crawl under the table and hide. Master these skills and you'll never fear fine dining again.

BIG FAT LIES WE TELL OURSELVES ABOUT WINE

Until now, you have been conning yourself about wine. Don't believe me? Then check out this list of commonly preconceived notions that tend to mess with the minds of wine beginners. In fact, even consumers who fancy themselves to be connoisseurs fall for these beliefs. You'll know better the next time you hear one.

1. "IF IT'S EXPENSIVE, IT'S GOT TO BE REALLY GOOD"

Economists like Robin Goldstein and Steven Levitt have made headlines by pointing out the fallacies in wine pricing. Their studies have shown that in blind tastings consumers don't enjoy expensive wines any more than they do cheap ones. Even experts can be hoodwinked: Put a bargain-priced wine in a decanter and they'll declare it to be of the finest quality. So don't assume that the $200 wine is necessarily "better" than the $15 bottle. It's different, sure, but it might not be to your taste. And its price is probably inflated, like that couture dress that doesn't really look all that different from the department store design.

2. "THE WINE WITH THE 99-POINT SCORE MUST BE WORTH THE SPLURGE"

Along the same lines, just because an influential critic rated a wine highly doesn't mean that you will love it. It doesn't even mean that the wine is unassailably good. Wine is like food—some people like it spicy, some people like it sweet. And pros who take notes on hundreds of wines a day might be seeking something different than consumers who just want to sip something simple after work. So don't take a critic's judgment as the final word on a wine. Also, keep in mind that high scores inflate prices.

3. "ALWAYS GO FOR THE 'RESERVE'"

In Italy, Spain, and Portugal, the terms "Riserva" or
"Reserva" indicate that the wine has aged in the winery
cellar for a specified amount of time. Elsewhere, the word
"Reserve" isn't regulated and thus doesn't mean much
when it's printed on a wine label. American wines
labeled Reserve tend to have more noticeable new oak,
concentrated fruit, bigger alcohol, and higher price
tags. If this kind of wine gives you a headache, why pay
more for it?

4. "ONLY DRINK GREAT VINTAGES"

It's a common misconception that we can't truly appreciate
wine without referring to a vintage chart, whatever that is.
But vintages deemed "great" by critics are those expected
to improve with decades of cellar age. Since most wines are
consumed within five years, most of us needn't concern
ourselves with this issue. Also, advances in viticulture and
winemaking in recent years have made vintage variation
much less noticeable.

5. "I KNOW I DON'T LIKE THAT STYLE OF WINE, SO I'M NOT GOING TO ORDER IT"

If I had a dollar for every time someone expressed an
unequivocally negative wine opinion, then later realized
that they were wrong, I'd be rich. You say you don't like
"sweet" wines? Spend some time tasting crisp Loire Chenin
Blanc or Mosel Riesling and you might want to rethink
that opinion. Not a fan of oak barrel aging? You might
be surprised to learn that many of the world's white and
red wines age in neutral, or used, barrels that impart no
perceptible aromas or flavors to the wine. Are you an
"anything but Chardonnay" drinker? Then maybe you
haven't tried Chablis.

COACHING FOR WINNING
THAT WINE LIST

If this writing career doesn't work out, I've got half a mind to become a wine-positive therapist because wine mastery is mostly a matter of working through our anxieties and approaching the subject with a relaxed, confident demeanor. So let's work on losing our hang-ups and inhibitions. Take a few deep breaths—that's right!—and join me ....

1. TAKE A LOAD OFF

Restaurants are businesses, and in a restaurant it's the job of the sommelier, wine director, or server to know the wine list. The onus isn't on *you* to be able to select a wine in seconds—it's on *them* to help you to navigate the list. That's what they get paid for, after all. So relieve yourself of that burden.

2. YOU DON'T HAVE TO KNOW EVERYTHING

Don't cram your brain full of extraneous information. Scores, vintages, châteaux, and appellations won't stick in your mind if they don't make sense to you. In chapters three and five you learned about a lot of different wine styles, countries, and regions. Just try to learn a few key facts about the wines that sound appealing to you and allow your curiosity and experience to take you from there.

If an insufferable loudmouth tries to spar with you by rattling off all the great wines he or she has bought or tasted, don't feel that you must respond by citing comparable experiences and encyclopedia entries. A good retort is, "I don't like to overanalyze my tasting experiences. I simply connect with wine on a sensory level."

3. IMPRESS BY ASKING QUESTIONS

For a wine professional, it's incredibly gratifying to guide customers through a journey of discovery, turning them onto a wine that they've never tried before. And it's absolutely stultifying to stand there listening to a blowhard lecture everyone about a wine that they may—*or may not*—be familiar with. So don't spout. Instead, inquire. The more questions you ask, the happier that wine merchant or sommelier will be. Oh, and don't worry about offending your server by asking for an inexpensive wine. Servers aren't exactly renowned for their fat paychecks, so they're a terrific resource for bang-for-the-buck recommendations.

4. REVERSE THE POWER STRUCTURE

Was that a wine list or a ticking time bomb that just landed in your hands? Everyone is watching and judging you as you flip through the pages … or at least, that's the way it feels. Well then, toss the grenade to someone else. Stall by asking your dining companions what they're eating and what sort of wine sounds good to them. Lob that ball right back to the server … what do *they* recommend?

5. BE CRAFTY AND EMPATHIC

Professional card champions run quick calculations in their heads while they're playing, assessing the odds. They read facial expressions, feign confidence, and deploy charm. You can use these tactics, too, when you're selecting wine. Because this isn't about you. It's about your companions and the dining experience you'll all be having together. How do they react when you mention certain wines? By assessing their responses to suggestions and smoothly replying to them, you'll be able to select a wine that balances out the desires of everyone at the table.

ROLE-PLAYING TYPICAL WINE SCENARIOS

White, red, or pink? Dry or sweet? Cheap, mid-range, or pricey? You can solve the time-honored dilemma of what to order simply by asking questions and narrowing the options down. So open that wine list, then turn to your companions or server and start asking questions. Let's walk through a few possible scenarios.

IN A WINE SHOP

You walk into a wine shop and are immediately overwhelmed. The place seems to be arranged geographically but there aren't any signs to point you toward any wine regions you know. Instead of panicking, engage.

TO THE MERCHANT *"Hi. I know I like Pinot Noir but I'd like to try something new. I've heard this is the place to come for superb recommendations. Can you direct me toward something delicious that might surprise me? I'm looking to spend about $20."*

WITH YOUR FRENEMY

You're at a hipper-than-thou boîte *where no one seems to be eating anything. You're with your chic frenemy, who works in fashion and has a knack for making you feel foolish. The wine list is printed on a piece of paper no larger than an index card and looks like secret passwords. Words are arranged in a single column with no explanation. Is this some sort of experimental art piece?*

Schell Mann "Gumpoldskirchen"
Dom de Saint Pierre
La Stoppa "Ageno"
Clos Fantine Faugeres Tradition
Act like you're awestruck by its minimalist beauty.

TO THE SERVER *"This list is so beautifully curated, it's to die for. What's inspiring you right now?"*

You're on a business boondoggle, the company is covering the bill, and the client wants red Bordeaux. You don't know squat about Bordeaux. But now isn't the time to admit that.

TO THE CLIENT *"Ah, you must have a terrific palate. What's your favorite château and vintage?*

CLIENT *"I do buy quite a bit of Pichon-Lalande. As for vintage, I just buy whatever my wine advisor tells me to."*

TO THE CLIENT *"Oh, I can never say it correctly. Can you repeat it? Your accent is impeccable. You must have studied French."*

The client repeats the name—you've got the pronunciation now, and you quickly come up with a way to remember it. But you have no idea whether it's on the wine list because when you were studying it, you just saw blurred lines of gobbledygook. And uh oh … time's run out. Here comes the sommelier.

TO THE SOMMELIER *"We'll be having the duck and the steak, and we'd like a Bordeaux. My companion here is a fan of Peach-un-la-land but it might be fun to try something else. What do you recommend?"*

....

You're on a date, you're treating, and your budget is tight. You don't want to order the first wine on the list just because it is the cheapest. But you'd really like to stay under $35 if you can without making it obvious that you're pinching pennies. When the server arrives to ask you for your wine order, hold the menu up and surreptitiously point to the first wine (it's $30) with your finger.

TO THE SERVER *"I'm looking for something along these lines. What's tasting delicious right now?"*

Your manager holds her cards close. You get the feeling she likes you, and you want to show her that you are up for taking on new challenges. On a business trip, you're out to dinner with your team. You reach for the wine list, beguiling everyone with your feigned assurance.

TO THE TEAM *"Well, there are six of us, so we may as well order a couple of bottles of wine. Hey, there's a rosé here. That might be fun … a taste of summer in November?"*

You glance around at everyone, making sure to notice your manager's response. She shrugs, frowning slightly.

TO THE TEAM *"Hmm, I'm not hearing a lot of enthusiasm. Okay, how about starting with a white?"*

Your manager lifts an eyebrow with a slight smile. Bingo. You rack your brain for what you know from reading this book. Now you remember: Chardonnay's true home is Burgundy, France, and Pinot Grigio's home is Friuli, northern Italy.

TO THE TEAM *"Raise your hand if you like a rich Chardonnay. Now raise your hand for Pinot Grigio. Looks like Pinot Grigio wins it, but I think we can order something more fun than that."*

TO THE SERVER, CONFIDENTLY *"We'll start with a light white as an aperitif. My esteemed colleagues here are fans of a light Friulian white, but what do you recommend?"*

Now for the next bottle. Your colleagues order chicken, fish and vegetarian dishes. You remember from chapter two that light reds like Pinot Noir go well with lighter meats and vegetable dishes.

TO THE TEAM *"I'm thinking a Pinot Noir would complement everyone's dinner. Has anyone tried an Oregon Pinot before?"*

Just because you like to cook, your prospective parents-in-law have the idea that you are some sort of wine expert. When the wine list arrives during the big meal out, they hand it to you and put you in charge. You don't want to insult them by spending too much money or ordering something they won't enjoy. So you ask everyone what style of wine they like, and—curses!—no one's on the same page.

TO THE IN-LAWS *"Hmm, we're all eating something very different, and we each have our own taste in wine. But I'll bet we can find something that we all like. How about we start with a bubbly—would everyone have a glass?"*

Everyone says that's a great idea. You order a bottle of the Prosecco, which isn't expensive. That should have pleased the white wine drinkers. And it bought you some time.

TO THE IN-LAWS *"Okay, for our main courses, could we go with a light-to-medium-bodied red wine? I'll bet we can find one that we all like."*

TO THE SERVER *"I'm looking at your reds and trying to find one that would fit with all of our meals. Something with good acidity and maybe a bit of spice?"*

WHAT DO ALL OF THESE SCENARIOS HAVE IN COMMON?

You have taken charge of the situation without getting bogged down in the details of wine speak. By listening and reacting, you've pleased your dining companions, complimented the good sense of your server or sommelier, and looked like a wine ninja.

Which you are. So own it.

Chapter Five

EMBRACE THE UNKNOWN

It's said that smart shoppers frequent the outskirts of the supermarket. Here, there are no shiny packages, no brand names, no unlimited shelf lives. Just humble, affordable fresh produce—the most high-quality and nutritious food in the building. Well, I'm going to let you in on a secret: Savvy wine consumers find the best deals in the obscure periphery of the bottle shop, where there are no big names, no point scores, and no high price tags.

EMBRACE OBSCURITY

We all know a jaded music snob who complains that his favorite band was "good until they sold out." Did the music quality really go downhill? Or is our friend just disappointed because that band is no longer a closely guarded secret and the price of concert tickets has increased exponentially? Either way, obscurity equals value.

Obscurity equals value. Industry insiders are always on the lookout for the next gritty, undiscovered wine find

Wine is the same way. Industry insiders are always on the lookout for the next gritty, undiscovered find. This could be one producer, or it could be an entire region, or a genre within a region. While their customers are splurging on big-name, high-scoring wines, sommeliers and merchants know that the more obscure the wine, the better the deal. For example, wine geeks tend not to buy "Grand Marque," or big-name, Champagnes. Instead, they go for the growers, or small family estates. While they're no longer a well-kept secret, these producers still tend to offer more bang for your buck than a large corporate Champagne house does.

Similarly, in Limoux, the world's oldest sparkling-wine region, a bubbly is made from the obscure Mauzac grape, in exactly the way Champagne is. But Limoux costs a lot less—less than $15 in most cases—because so few people are familiar with the appellation and the grape. The world is filled with pockets of pleasure like this. The further you venture off the beaten track, the more rewarding the experience will be. There's a Lebanese wine that's a dead ringer for classic Bordeaux and a red from the Republic of Macedonia that tastes like it should cost four times what it does.

Even if you feel like a wine ignoramus—and you don't need to memorize every page of chapter three—you can play this game. Start lurking around the remote corners of wine shops. On restaurant wine lists, look for the "Other" heading that comes after France, Italy, Spain, etc.

Opposite: Grand Marque Champagne is a treat, but grower Champagne offers better bang for the buck

MEET THE OUTLIERS

In chapter three, we covered the basics as well as many lesser-known finds—like Limoux and Lagrein—in the world's top wine-producing nations. But there is so much more out there! To give you a taste, here are a few nations that, for the most part, offer fantastic value because they're well-kept secrets:

CROATIA

Just as tourists have discovered Croatia's beaches in recent years, they have also stumbled upon its sophisticated wine industry, most notably in the northern peninsula-and-island region of Istria on the eastern shore of the Gulf of Venice. Smooth golden whites lead the pack here, from grapes like Malvazija (the Croatian way to say Malvasia) and Graševina, known as Welschriesling in Austria and Germany. Croatia's other two key wine regions are the Dalmatian Coast and Slavonia, the birthplace of Slavonian oak barrels.

Croatia, a popular vacation getaway, has a sophisticated wine industry

CYPRUS

A winemaking goliath of the ancient world is today an ethnically divided Mediterranean island notable only for Commandaria, a sweet, tawny fortified wine. However, outside investors, a renewed interest in native grape varieties, and a doubling down on quality in recent years suggest that the Cypriots might be the next darlings of the wine scene.

GEORGIAN REPUBLIC

Archaeological evidence suggests that the nation of Georgia was the birthplace of winemaking. Decades of Soviet rule suppressed quality wine production here, but today, artisanal producers are re-emerging and vinifying wines from a fascinating array of indigenous grapes. Instead of barrels or tanks, the most interesting winemakers are using traditional *qvevri*, which are giant underground vessels molded from terracotta. It may take a few sips to get used to flavor and texture of these wines, but the happy sommelier will be talking your ear off while you're acclimating your palate.

Grapevines thrive in the high-altitude hillside vineyards of sunny Cyprus

Lebanon's Bekaa Valley is known for its Greco-Roman ruins and elegant wines

As you begin to explore the world of wine outsiders, get in the habit of turning the bottle around and looking for the name of the importer.

LEBANON

Another country with a long winemaking history behind it, Lebanon produces excellent wine despite its location in the middle of a geopolitical hot zone. Vineyards are clustered in the Bekaa Valley and French grape varieties from Bordeaux and the Rhône predominate, but some native grapes are showing great promise.

REPUBLIC OF MACEDONIA

Again, a historic wine region boasting its own index of indigenous grapes with titles that sound like newly patented medications. Vranec doesn't cure the flu, but it does cure general malaise, and as I type this, there is an excellent bottle available in my city for $11. Alas, just across the border from the nation of Macedonia is the region of Macedonia in Greece. Fortunately for us, the Greek wine labels tend to be printed with the names of smaller sub-zones, alleviating the confusion.

SLOVENIA

If you haven't gotten the message by now, the Balkans are back. And among the Balkans, Slovenia has prime placement. Its westernmost wine region is its biggest star, but what to call it in this multilingual nation? It's "Primorska" in Slovenian, but it also goes by Littoral or Primorje, depending on the context. The Brda sub-zone shares a porous border with northeastern Italy's Friuli, and grapes and winemaking styles straddle both sides. And in the northeastern corner of Slovenia, Podravje, bordering Austria, Hungary, and Croatia, is a large area producing excellent wines.

> **INSIDER TIP:** IMPORTERS ARE CURATORS
>
> As you begin to explore the world of outsider wines, get in the habit of looking for the name of the importer on the back labels of your favorite wine finds. Over time, you'll be able to walk into a bottle shop and make an informed decision merely by turning the bottle around and seeing who found the producer and shipped the wine.

Slovenia's Goriska Brda wine region borders Friuli, Italy

EXTRA CREDIT

Finally, let's meet the emerging markets. The following nations and states produce wines that are nearly impossible to find outside of their home borders. In some cases, the industries are so new that quality can be uneven. But keep an eye on them all the same. In a couple of decades, we may all be buying Chinese wine.

CHINA
The world's biggest economy has a voracious appetite for wine. Its fast-growing industry focuses on Bordeaux varieties; and although much is produced, very little is exported.

INDIA
India's massive economy, too, is supporting an upstart winemaking industry, but it's nearly impossible to taste the fruits of its efforts, since few bottles are shipped overseas.

ISRAEL
The Galilee wine region—in particular, the Golan Heights—is breaking out with wines that don't taste like that kosher plonk that historically has plagued Jewish households on holidays. Bordeaux-style red blends, in particular, are finding fans of every faith.

The new wave of Chinese wines are sold in glass bottles, not ceramic pots

LATIN AMERICA
Brazil, Mexico, and Uruguay are all emerging as fine wine-producing nations. Most notably, some critics believe that Uruguayan Tannat is better than the reds of Madiran, the grape's stronghold in Southwest France.

LUXEMBOURG
Some lovely white and sparkling wines are made in this nation, but it's smaller than Rhode Island, so we don't get to taste them very often. The vineyards follow the banks of the Moselle River, which becomes the Mosel when it crosses the border into Germany.

MOROCCO
In recent years, foreign investors and French winemakers have been moving into this former Gallic colony in North Africa. The red Carignan and Cinsault are the most widely planted grapes, and they make some nice rosés as well.

TURKEY
Governmental restrictions and taxes on alcohol sales have challenged Turkey's wine industry, and very few of its wines are exported. However, visiting tourists are delighted to find intriguing bottles, the most interesting of which are vinified from native grape varieties.

THE LESSER-KNOWN USA

Arizona
Rhône red varieties, such as Syrah, are attracting attention in the Grand Canyon state.

Idaho
California, Oregon, and Washington have proven that the Pacific Coast favors wine production. Inland Idaho is quietly joining its neighbors, establishing a reputation for Riesling and a variety of reds.

New Mexico
Gruet sparkling wines are a staple on wine lists all over the nation. What's next for this high-elevation state?

Texas
Don't mess with the leathery, savory reds of Texas, which take their cues from Rioja, the Rhône Valley, and Bordeaux.

Virginia
While mom-and-pop establishments still dominate here, a handful of wineries aim to break away from the folksy stereotype, most successfully with plush Bordeaux-style red blends.

> Wine merchants have great respect for adventurous customers who frequent the outer edges of the bottle shop.

Chapter Six

LEARN THE LINGO

Wine language can be opaque, bizarre, and, with a surprising amount of frequency, unintentionally and ridiculously carnal. It would be perfectly reasonable to say, "That 555 clone gets so big with too much skin contact. And look at the legs on it! It's silky, but hot." We'll begin by learning general terms related to winemaking and appreciation. Then we'll pick apart some of the most opaque descriptors that critics use in tasting notes.

A SELECT LIST OF TASTING TERMS

Just as you should hear a slang phrase in action before you launch it off yourself, these terms need context to be fully understood. So hang out at tastings, read wine publications, or watch a bunch of YouTube clips to get a feel for the way these words are used. Once you feel comfortable, toss a few of them out in a winery tasting room and see what happens. You will feel so money. You will feel wickedly good.

ACID
A hallucinogen for people, a pick-me-up for wine. It's what makes your mouth water for another sip.

BALANCE
Essential in wine as well as circus performers. In wine, the big three—acid, tannin, and fruit—should always be balanced so that you don't notice any one of these properties more than the others.

BIG
Bottles as huge as helium tanks are physically big. A "big wine" is flavorfully big, with tons of color, flavor, alcohol, and tannin. Synonyms include powerful and robust.

BODY
A corpse. Also, a way to describe the density of a wine. Light-bodied wines are lower in alcohol and watery. Full-bodied wines are higher in alcohol and syrupy.

BOUQUET
I have used this word in wine descriptions in the past, and I'm not proud of it. It's a priggish way of introducing a long list of all the different aromas you can smell and everyone else can't.

CHEWY
Chewbacca would totally love chewy wines. They're

full-bodied reds with enough tannins that you almost feel like you could chew them.

CLOSED

Some temperamental wines just close for business for a few hours, days, or even years and then re-open. The bummer is, they don't put a sign over the shop window to let you know in advance when they are going to do this. So if you open a perennial favorite and it tastes blah, don't give up on that particular wine. Another bottle might be yummy in another week or year or two. Yes, I did just use the term "yummy."

CONCENTRATED

A wine as dense as frozen juice concentrate that's only been mixed with half the recommended amount of water. Synonyms include fat, extracted, and jammy.

DRY

I don't understand how this word can mean both the opposite of sweet and the opposite of wet, but it does.

DUSTY

This is a texture term, referring to tannins that are light on your tongue like powdered sugar rather than harsh like steel wool.

FINISH

The flavors that linger in your mouth after you've swallowed. A quality wine should have a long, complex finish. A short finish is a bummer.

FIRM

No two wine critics would define this word the same way. As far as I can tell, it means tough, but not too tough. "Hard tannins" are fiercer than "firm tannins." Both terms imply that the wine could use some cellar-age or aeration to soften and smooth out those tannins.

FLABBY
A body part that is all cushion, no muscle tone. A wine that's all fruit, no acidity.

HOT
So high in alcohol that you feel like a fire-breathing dragon when you exhale after taking a sip.

JAZZY
No, wine can't do jazz hands. It can't scat, swing a walking baseline, or improvise a trumpet solo. While jazzy can mean "gaudy" in a visual context, critics don't tend to use this word to imply that a wine is over-the-top. Rather, jazzy implies a sense of liveliness in the mouth, with blasts of fruit flavor.

MINERALITY
Do rocks have a taste or smell? If you put a pebble in your mouth (wash it first) or sit by a rocky stream, you'd agree that they do. Minerality also might have a bit of a matte texture to it.

MOUTHFEEL
The way the wine feels in your mouth. Duh. Two personal faves in the mouthfeel category are "spritzy," like lightly sparkling water, or smooth and "silky."

NOSE
In general, "on the nose" means obvious. In wine speak, aromas are described as "on the nose" in an effort to be as not-obvious as possible. It's uncouth for a wine critic to just, plain and simple, write that a wine "smells like" something. Because that would be too on-the-nose.

OAKY
Wine can ferment and age in oak and not smell oaky. Oaky wine has that burnt-caramel aroma that comes from newly toasted barriques. When critics get tired of using this word, they type "woody" instead.

POWERFUL
High in alcohol and ready to kick your ass.

TANNIN
Grape skins and seeds, as well as oak barrels, give wines that dry feeling like you're sucking on cotton balls or the inside of a banana peel. Apparently tannins are good for longevity, but in the short term they can be brutal.

GEEK SPEAK

Next time you're out, impress your dining companions by whipping out one of these bad boys.

ABV
The fine print on the label that lists the Alcohol by Volume (ABV) matters. It's possible to sip 11%ABV Vinho Verde all afternoon in the hot sun and be perfectly fine, but open a 14.5%ABV with dinner the next night and end up with a pounding headache. Also, there's wiggle room in labeling laws, so that 14.5% wine might actually be 15.5%. Just saying.

ACIDITY
This book blathers on a lot about the importance of cool breezes and high elevations. That's because, unless grape ripeness is counterbalanced by acidity, the resulting wine will be a short-lived dud. The winemaker can add acid to correct this problem, but it's preferable to achieve acidity naturally, in the vineyard.

AERATE
Do you need a decanter? No. But some wines do benefit from exposure to air. For example, powerful reds that are dark in color generally will benefit from sitting in the glass and "breathing." So if you're having guests over to dinner, just pour the red while you're setting the table. By the time everyone sits down, it will be in top form.

AMPHORA

Yes, you read that right. Amphorae are back. They're huge terracotta vessels that allow for a bit of oxygen transfer during fermenting and aging without imparting flavor. The oldest type of clay winemaking vessel known to archaeologists is the *qvevri*, still in use today in the Republic of Georgia.

APPELLATION

Here's the secret to understanding wine: 1) place is all-important; 2) wine experts are obsessed with putting things into categories. An appellation hits both marks: It's the official name for a geographic area designated by officials to be important for wine production. Which is a lah-dee-dah way of saying that it's the name of a wine region. See also the next entry.

AVA

In the United States, appellations are called American Viticultural Areas. They're the place names, such as Napa Valley, that appear on wine labels. In Europe, appellations are DOC(G), DO, and other acronyms. In France, AOC is currently transitioning to AOP, and the rest of Europe is scheduled to follow suit soon. Which is not A-OK for someone who just memorized the old appellation system.

BARREL AGE

Wines age in barrels for months or even years prior to release. Since new barrels are expensive and take up valuable space at the winery, these wines are pricier than those sold soon after harvest.

BARREL FERMENTATION

Barrel fermentation is rarer than barrel aging. The process of juice turning to wine usually happens in a stainless-steel tank or a big cement vat. It's thought that fermentation in a giant wooden barrel or cask softens the wine's texture because of the gentle oxygen transfer that happens through the pores of the wood.

BARRIQUE

A small French barrel used for aging that can impart lots of flavor and texture to wine, especially if it has been toasted (lightly charred) over a flame and is brand-new. However, a new barrique doesn't necessarily turn wine into a burnt-caramel parfait. Barrels that have been air-dried or steamed, not toasted, make mellow wines.

BLIND TASTING

Sadly, nothing like Pin the Tail on the Donkey or *50 Shades of Grey*. Because the bottles, not you, are the ones wearing the blindfolds; they're hidden in paper bags (or whatever is available). If you want to get all *Rain Man* and try to blind-identify a wine by variety, region, producer, vintage, and vineyard, good for you. But contrary to popular opinion, blind tasting is really just a tool to keep us from making assumptions about a wine before we taste it.

BLOCK

A small defined section of a vineyard, sometimes noted on a wine label.

BODEGA

The Spanish term for a winery. Also, a stop-and-shop on a busy New York City street where you can buy cigarettes, chips, and undrinkable coffee.

BOTTLE AGE

When wine is transferred from a porous barrel to an airtight bottle, it can freak out and temporarily go into "bottle shock," which sounds like the name of a punk band. This is one of the many reasons wineries bottle-age their wines prior to selling them. Labeling regulations of some wine regions require a specific period of bottle aging at the winery prior to release.

BRIX

A measure of sugar in grapes. A high brix number doesn't

necessarily translate into a sweet wine, as sugar is converted into alcohol during fermentation. Also, the name for a building material in the *Asterix* comic books.

CAVE
A cavity in a rock cliff where bears hibernate and prehistoric people painted crazy scenes just to mess with the minds of future anthropologists. When it's pronounced *KAHV* (in French), it's the word for a cellar where barrels and bottles are stored.

CLONE
Dolly the Sheep. Dudes in white body armor in the *Stars Wars* franchise. Also, a specific strain of a grape variety, such as Pinot Noir. Clones can be the result of spontaneous mutation, which sounds totally sci-fi. Today they are propagated mostly in nurseries, which is less interesting. Vineyard owners try to plant the clones that will thrive in their location and climate.

CLOS
Pronounced *KLOH*, this is a fancy French vineyard surrounded by a stone wall, which makes the vines outside the wall feel bad about themselves.

COMMUNE
Where naked hippies live and love. When pronounced *KUH-moon*, it's a top wine-producing village in France.

CONCRETE
Concrete fermentation tanks have been used forever in Europe because they're indestructible and tend to stay nice and cool. The new, chic concrete tanks are molded into weird shapes, which supposedly make the wine better.

CRU
A very special vineyard or grouping of vineyards.

In Burgundy, the best crus are "Grand" and the second-best are "Premier." In Bordeaux, the best are called "Premier," or spelled "1er," Cru designations are printed on labels so that wineries can charge more. Er, I mean, so that consumers can identify wines of the highest quality.

CRUSH
The worst part about eighth grade. Also, the stressful make-it-or-break-it period just after harvest when the fermentation is supposed to go smoothly but doesn't, no one at the winery gets any sleep, and everyone drinks a lot of beer.

CUVÉE
A blend of different grapes either all of the same variety but from numerous vineyards, or of numerous varieties. Incidentally, many bottles labeled with just one grape variety actually contain a little bit of another type of grape that's been added as a seasoning.

FERMENTATION
The magical process that turns juice into wine. It requires sugar (in the form of fruit), yeast, patience, and fairy dust. Also, as previously noted, beer.

FIELD BLEND
Back in the days of yore, vineyards were often jumbles of different grape varieties and clones and no one bothered figuring out what was what. The resulting wine was, in essence, blended in the field rather than in the tank or barrel. These days, there's a certain old-fashioned charm to a field blend.

FINING/FILTERING
Processes that remove impurities from wine prior to bottling. Some enthusiasts claim that unfined and unfiltered wines are more natural and therefore superior, but it all depends on the wine and the vintage.

GRAPE NAMES VS. PLACE NAMES

Major stumbling block for wine newcomers. In Europe, wines are usually labeled by place, not grape. It's just assumed that you know that red wine labeled "Bourgogne" (Burgundy) is Pinot Noir. Because what are you, a cretin? In the New World, the name of the grape usually appears on the label, since there aren't legal restrictions on what variety of grape is grown where.

HORIZONTAL VS. VERTICAL FLIGHT

In winetasting, a horizontal is a group of wines all from the same vintage, and a vertical is a group of wines from successive vintages.

LATE HARVEST

"We had a late harvest that year" means that the growing season was cold and it took longer than usual for the grapes to ripen. "It's a late-harvest wine" means that the winemaker left the grapes on the vine late into fall or early winter, allowing them to shrivel into sweet raisins for dessert wine production.

LEGS/TEARS

Tears flow when kids fall down and skin their legs on the sidewalk. But when drops of liquid ooze down the inside of a wine glass slowly, that wine's got legs, which means it's high in alcohol and/or sugar.

MALOLACTIC FERMENTATION

Goes by the handle "malo," or "ML". It's a secondary fermentation that converts astringent malic acid into soft lactic acid. Red wines generally go through malo. Crisp whites don't, but softer whites, like many Chardonnays, do. Along with barrel-age and lees stirring (see Sur Lie, p.218), malolactic fermentation is what makes many Chardonnays so buttery-soft.

MASSAL SELECTION

A survival-of-the-fittest, DIY way of planting new vines.

Instead of buying genetically identical clones from a nursery (reminder—we're talking plants here, not human babies), the vinetender snips shoots off the healthiest vines already established in the vineyard and propagates those. This is time-consuming but makes for more genetic diversity and, arguably, a better match between plant and site. If you want to sound really French, say "*selection massale*."

NATIVE YEAST
Winemakers can add yeast to start fermentation, or they can wait around for native (also known as "wild" or "indigenous") yeast spores to settle in and do their thing.

NÉGOCIANT
Négociants buy excess inventory (fruit, juice, or finished wine) from other wineries and blend and bottle their own wines, which can be terrific value.

NEUTRAL OAK
Barrels used for three or four years no longer add woody, smoky, spicy, or sweet notes to wine and are described as "neutral." Neutral oak imparts a silky texture without adding a noticeably woody aroma and flavor. Air-dried and steamed new barrels are a happy medium between toasty new oak and neutral oak.

ROOTSTOCK
In the nineteenth century, Americans inadvertently brought an icky little vine louse called *phylloxera* to Europe. (Please don't hate us, Europe.) Said louse went postal on Europe's vineyards until it was discovered that the European vines could be grafted onto tough American roots, aka rootstock. Like the bouncers outside Studio 54, American rootstock keeps the nasty little leeches away from the nobility.

RS
The residual sugar left over after fermentation is complete. If the acidity is high enough to balance out

the RS, the wine will taste dry. Also, be warned—if you overindulge in a wine with a fairly high ABV (above 14%) and RS (above three grams/liter), you can pretty much bank on waking up with a headache tomorrow. So sip that Port slowly and beware high-alcohol wines that also taste slightly sweet.

SKIN CONTACT

It sounds sexy. Alas, it's just another term for maceration, or that time period when the grape juice and skins are still all mingled together. Skin contact imparts color, flavor, and tannins to wine.

SUB-APPELLATION

A wine region within a wine region. Like Russian dolls, there can be sub-appellations inside sub-appellations inside sub-appellations. In this book, I've largely used the word "sub-zone" because the word "zone" makes a lot more sense to wine newbies.

SULFITES

Sulfur dioxide is an insect/mildew deterrent in the vineyard and prevents spoilage in a finished wine. If you get headaches, try a lower-alcohol wine before declaring yourself "allergic to sulfites" because there are a lot of other foods that would bother you if you truly had a problem with sulfur. Nonetheless, there are wines that don't contain sulfites that you can try if you think you're sulfur sensitive.

SUR LIE

The attitude of a spoiled teenager. Also, the French way of saying "on the lees." Spent yeast lees settle at the bottom of wine barrels. Winemakers either "rack" (remove) them, or leave them in the barrel, stirring them occasionally, so that certain wines take on their soft texture and creamy flavor. *Battonage* is the French term for stirring lees. It may also be a way to describe the twilight years of bats, or an orphanage for lost baseball and cricket bats.

TERROIR

The wine equivalent of holding a conch shell to your ear and hearing the sea. If you think you can taste or smell the place where the grapes were grown, you can say a wine exhibits excellent terroir.

VARIETAL

A *variety* is a type of grape, such as Riesling or Syrah. A *varietal* is a wine made from a single grape variety. So a bottle labeled "Syrah" contains a varietal wine. A bottle labeled "Red Blend" does not.

VINTAGE

The year in which a wine was harvested. Harvest occurs in the autumn and wines generally aren't released until the next spring or later. In the southern hemisphere, the seasons are reversed, so harvest might happen in March instead of September. But you knew that.

WHOLE-CLUSTER

Instead of running them through a crusher-destemmer machine, the winemaker drops the whole intact grape clusters into the fermentation tank or press. Whole-cluster, also called whole bunch winemaking, can be costly, time-consuming, and risky, but winemakers who practice it say they get a smoother, spicier wine.

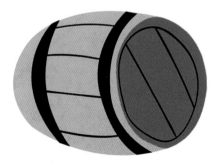

INDEX

ACKNOWLEDGMENTS & DEDICATION

Sterling approved the plans for this book. Quarto constructed it.

Hilary Lumsden and John Round did all the heavy lifting. (I hope they are drinking something delicious right now.)

And now I get to dedicate it.

First, to my friends, who think I know everything about wine.

Second, to the wine professionals, who know that no one has all the answers.

Third, to my parents, for whom wine is a way of experiencing life.

Most of all, to my husband and daughters, with whom life is a joyous experience.

REFERENCES

Asimov, Eric, *How to Love Wine: A Memoir and Manifesto* (New York, William Morrow, 2012)

Baiocchi, Talia, *Sherry: A Modern Guide to the World's Best-Kept Secret, with Cocktails and Recipes* (Berkeley, Ten Speed Press, 2014)

Bonné, John, *The New California Wine: A Guide to the Producers and Wines Behind a Revolution in Taste* (Berkeley, Ten Speed Press, 2013)

Clarke, Oz, *Oz Clarke Pocket Wine A-Z* (London, Pavilion Books, 2014)

Goode, Jamie, *The Science of Wine: From Vine to Glass* (Berkeley, University of California Press, 2014)

Johnson, Hugh, *Hugh Johnson's Pocket Wine Book* (London, Mitchell Beazley, 2015)

Lukacs, Paul, *Inventing Wine: A New History of One of the World's Most Ancient Pleasures* (New York, W.W. Norton & Co., 2013)

MacNeil, Karen, *The Wine Bible* (New York, Workman Publishing, 2015)

Murphy, Linda, and Robinson, Jancis, *American Wine: The Ultimate Companion to the Wines and Wineries of the United States* (Berkeley, University of California Press, 2014)

Pigott, Stuart, *Best White Wine on Earth: The Riesling Story* (New York, Stewart, Tabori & Chang, 2014)

BIBLIOGRAPHY

Bastianich, Joseph, and Lynch, David, *Vino Italiano: The Regional Wines of Italy* (New York, Clarkson Potter, 2005)

Coates, Clive, *An Encyclopedia of the Wines and Domaines of France* (Berkeley, University of California Press, 2000)

Cole, Katherine, Complete *Wine Selector: How to Choose the Right Wine Every Time* (Toronto, Firefly Books, 2013)

D'Agata, Ian, *Native Wine Grapes of Italy* (Berkeley, University of California Press, 2014)

Foer, Joshua, *Moonwalking with Einstein: The Art and Science of Remembering Everything* (New York, Penguin, 2011)

Halliday, James, *Wine Atlas of Australia* (Berkeley, University of California Press, 2006)

Johnson, Hugh, and Robinson, Jancis, *The World Atlas of Wine* (London, Mitchell Beazley, 2001)

Kramer, Matt, *Matt Kramer on Wine: A Matchless Collection of Columns, Essays, and Observations by America's Most Original and Lucid Wine Writer* (New York, Sterling Epicure, 2010)

Phillips, Rod, *Alcohol: A History* (Chapel Hill, The University of North Carolina Press, 2014)

Robinson, Jancis, editor, *The Oxford Companion to Wine* (Oxford, Oxford University Press, 1999)

PICTURE CREDITS

Every effort has been made to trace all copyright owners but if any have been inadvertently overlooked, the publishers would be pleased to make the necessary arrangements at the first opportunity. (Key: **t** = Top, **b** = Bottom, **c** = Center, **tl** = top left, **tr** = top right, **cl** = center left, **cr** = center right, **bl** = bottom left, **br** = bottom right)